ALAN SILLITOE

Raw Material

GRAFTON BOOKS

A Division of the Collins Publishing Group

LONDON GLASGOW
TORONTO SYDNEY AUCKLAND

Grafton Books
A Division of the Collins Publishing Group
8 Grafton Street, London W1X 3LA

Published by Grafton Books 1987

First published in Great Britain by
W. H. Allen & Co Ltd 1972

Copyright © Alan Sillitoe 1972, 1974, 1978

ISBN 0-586-06565-2

Printed and bound in Great Britain by
Collins, Glasgow

Set in Times

Al[...] t fourteen
to [...] air traffic
co[..] Production
in [.......]

He enlisted in May 1940 into the RAF VR, and spent two
years on active service in Malaya as a wireless operator. At
the end of 1949 he was invalided out of the service with a
hundred per cent disability pension.

He began writing, and lived for six years in France and
Spain. His first stories were published in the *Notting-
ham-shire Weekly Guardian*. In 1958 *Saturday Night and Sunday
Morning* was published, and *The Loneliness of the Long-
distance Runner*, which won the Hawthornden Prize for
literature, came out the following year. Both these books
were made into films.

Further works include *Key to the Door*, *The Ragman's
Daughter* and *The General* (both also filmed), *The William
Posters Trilogy*, *A Start in Life*, *The Widower's Son*, *The
Second Chance* – as well as six volumes of poetry. His latest
books are *The Lost Flying Boat*, *Down from the Hill* and
Life Goes On. With his wife, Ruth Fainlight, he divides his
time between London and a house in Kent.

By the same author

Fiction

*Saturday Night and
   Sunday Morning*
*The Loneliness of the Long-
   distance Runner*
The General
Key to the Door
The Ragman's Daughter
A Tree on Fire
Guzman, Go Home
A Start in Life
Travels in Nihilon
Men, Women and Children
*The Death of William
   Posters*
The Flame of Life
The Widower's Son
The Storyteller
The Second Chance
Her Victory
The Lost Flying Boat
Down from the Hill
Life Goes On

Poetry

The Rats and Other Poems
*A Falling Out of Love and
   Other Poems*
*Love in the Environs of
   Voronezh*
Storm and Other Poems
*Snow on the North Side of
   Lucifer*
Sun Before Departure

Plays

All Citizens Are Soldiers
   (with Ruth Fainlight)
Three Plays

Non-Fiction

Road to Volgograd

Essays

Mountains and Caverns

For children

*The City Adventures of
   Marmalade Jim*
Big John and the Stars
*The Incredible Fencing
   Fleas*
Marmalade Jim on the Farm
Marmalade Jim and the Fox

'All the future is foretold, but freedom of choice is given to everyone.'

RABBI AKIBA BEN JOSEPH

PART ONE

I

In the beginning was the word, and Adam was the Printer's Devil.

As a boy I walked into the middle of Nottingham, passing St Barnabas' Cathedral on my way down Derby Road. In a deep niche of its grey-black wall sat a man with no legs, selling matches. The niche had a heavy wooden door to it, and he could lock the place securely every night before going home.

At the time of packing up I saw him put the money into his pocket without counting it – as if he had already noted every penny that dropped there during his long day. Then he folded the mat and set it at the back of the niche with his stock of matches. After a look to see that everything was tidy he came on to the pavement and locked the door. He propelled himself down the road by his two hands, the trousers of his brown suit pinned under his trunk. He wore a collar and tie, which somehow saddened his look of respectability.

His brown eyes watched people walking by all day long, and his single great indisputable truth was that the rest of the world had legs. He was privileged in having such an enormous and satisfying fact all to himself, but what a price he had had to pay for it. His features were a prison wall that held his thoughts and everything he suffered. He smiled, but never talked.

His fate did not seem so terrible to me as I now think it was. He had a way of earning a living, shelter from the rain while doing it, and a fact about himself with which he could gainsay every other truth. I did not envy him, but in my simplicity as a child I realised that his truth would have been absolute if only he had given into it entirely by staying in his wall-cave during the night as well.

When I asked my parents how he had lost his legs my mother said he'd been run over by a tram as a boy. My father told me they had been blown from under him twenty years before at the Battle of the Somme. My grandmother heard he'd been born like that. Grandfather Burton thought it as good a way as any to dodge his share of proper work.

It was difficult to know which of these tales to believe, but they ceased to matter after a while. The man still had no legs, after all.

2

The man with no legs is the first thing that comes to me as I start to write. There is much more, because this book is called *Raw Material*, part novel, part autobiography, but all in all a book, a reading book, and non-committal in these aspects till I get to the end. It is an attempt at self-portrait in which I will leave out the expected run-throughs of the confessional because I assume that most have been used, suitably disguised or not, in novels and stories already finished.

In any case, my plain unblemished life-story would in no way guarantee an accurate design, because the ordinary occurrences since birth may be weighed down by the heavy blight of lost happenings that took up my parents or grandparents. The important particulars that moved them, if one can sort it out from this point on in time, may be more vital than the petty issues I have been involved in.

Those events which were overwhelming and decisive may account for my inability to wear a simple necktie, indicating that some criminal antecedent was hanged for stealing a sheep, when a Celtic judge from my father's side did for some Jutish marauder on my mother's – or vice versa, since both strands are inextricably ravelled. Or perhaps I don't flash a tie because I am a rationalist and see no reason for it, or that it does not keep me warm and is therefore useless in the long run. If one sticks to the truth, all minor reasons need considering.

No matter what I call this book, I know it to be a novel after all, because everything written is fiction, even non-fiction – which may be the most fictional non-fiction of all. Under that heading are economic reports, international treaties, news items, Hansard accounts, biographies of 'great people', historical blow-by-blows of crises and military campaigns. Anything which is not scientific or mathematical fact is coloured by the human imagination and feeble opinion.

Fiction is a pattern of realities brought to life by suitably applied lies, and one has to be careful, in handling the laws of fiction, not to get so close to the truth that what is written loses its air of reality.

It is a hard test sailing so near the gale, but however this narrative is classified it bears no relationship either to golden truth or black lies. To pursue truth one minute while denying there is any such thing the next has the advantage of realism. Such vacillation divides the compulsively verbal persuaders from the writer who has neither time nor learning to swing anybody. For the talkers there is only one truth, and they know it. They go on talking so long that it stokes them up and keeps their home fires burning. Continual and maniac speech prevents self-knowledge and the threat of facing the wasteland. As a way of taking in air, it inflates them and keeps the feet just that bit above the earth to maintain their confidence. Politicians are so good at telling lies that their faces are not even pock-marked to show they are not being deceived by them.

On the other hand those who see truth everywhere have great difficulty in selecting certain truths to make a pattern of wisdom from it. Language becomes more precious when truths proliferate. It is not so easy then to talk or write, for truth is difficult to pin down when it is everywhere. But those who exult in the *truth* turn into a river of semantic devastation.

No one can speak for anyone else, and whoever says differently is a mean-throated, twin-faced liar. Perhaps I am saying that only God can speak the truth, which may or may not be a useful yardstick, because though it invites chaos in by the front door if one does not believe in God, one can only explore that chaos and reduce it to some ordered arrangement by a strict pursuit of truth regarding one's own attitude – so as to get out of the back door before the house falls in on both truth and lies together.

Having stated this, it seems unlikely at the moment that I shall ever get any truth from myself. But in case it becomes even more difficult in the future, through accident or loss of nerve, I had better attempt to do so now and get it over with, set my arms flailing and make a snatch at the truth with one or the other when any recognition of it seems possible in the distorting fog.

3

Outside on the window-ledge a wasp stings a fly into unconsciousness and walks off with it under its arm like a parcel.

A few minutes later, a mistle-thrush waddles back across the grass from chasing a sparrow, and the way the bird moves I know she has an egg in her. The same sights could be seen a hundred years ago, and at any time since.

I sit at a table in my room, dreaming of far-off places, of vultures making clouds of letters in the sky, black against blue, cutting up the sun with scissor-wings. They turn and spin, swoop and spit their deepest bile at a tree that is still burning, ignited by the sun whose hot rays pierce to the earth as soon as the vultures move down and away from it and are no longer its shadow.

Each of my two eyes is a door that has locks but no keys, and I burst open each in turn to go through and see what they will show me. Sometimes it is landscape, now and again it is people; often empty sky.

I live in a Kent village eight miles from the English sea, and wonder at my reasons for buying this house. It is an equal distance from Dover and Newhaven, so that I can get out of the country and on to the mainland with little delay, as well as being fifteen minutes from Lydd Airport in case a lightning getaway is called for.

I long for a bridge to be built over the Channel or a tunnel dug under it to France so that I can drive as far as China without touching water. Better still if the Channel were filled in, and this island was connected to the mainland which is its rightful place, all the rubbish of Europe tipped into the sea until land joins land and cliff meets cliff. Two ample canals could be built through it for ships, and that would be that.

The house is set in the comparatively fresh air of the countryside, though I can get to London in under two hours, and stand in Oxford Street choking thankfully on petrol fumes. It is so strategically placed that the built-up mass of London blocks me off from my past and family in Nottinghamshire. Perhaps I came here simply to write *Raw Material* – a tale of two Nottingham families shattered by the Empedoclean progress of the Great War, which may be the same as saying that they were broken by life itself.

But there were other reasons as I studied the map, though some of them seem wrong-headed now, as to why I chose the house I did. Certainly I don't write better or worse here than anywhere else, which is all that matters. There is enough space for me to accumulate quantities of books. When my eyes want to wander over the shelves I begin to wonder which I would abandon if I had to leave and could only take fifty with me, or whether I would worry overmuch if I had to clear out with none at all. It is a hypothetical though frequent question, being so close to the coast.

The few square miles of high land the village stands on are surrounded by marshes which are so flooded when the rains come that Oxney is again almost the island it once was in the Middle Ages. Acres of water on every side lap the borders of the few roads leading out from the island. Swans that float on it take off with a great fanning of wings and wild melancholy honkings that echo across the open spaces. Ink clouds reflected in the water remind me of the early morning rice fields outside Valencia.

In spring and autumn the sunsets are broad layers of snake-green and ox-blood on either side of Wittersham church tower, with no disturbing noise except for the occasional car. The colours are so thick and livid with tranquillity it seems I have only to reach beyond the bedroom window and peel them off in layers. But peace begets the opposite of truth, which cannot be found behind the deadening tints of a country dusk slowly torn apart by the flitting of numerous birds.

When frost comes the bushes and trees of the garden change from green to white. Even the smallest detail of leaves and grass blades shows up in the hoar frost. A freezing mist holds the patterns in their monochromatic place. By the end of the day it is like looking into a tank of milk, and I draw the curtains across it.

If the temperature rises slightly it brings white banks of snow lifting against the doors. But the house is solid and warm, a fit haven to deceive any man who thinks of getting the truth from it. He can sit there and ponder, knowing that when the snow melts he will be able to smell the earth again and find a little measure of truth and beauty in that, though never enough to satisfy.

All might be revealed if one goes back into the jungle, but the truth – never. Before a novelist comes into the open he must first find some trick of getting inside himself, and there is no other way to do it but go backwards, which is the only direction left if one is to rediscover the fictional truth that sprawls behind one's spirit.

4

If I am tempted to say that nothing I have so far written has been of the truth, it is only so that I can question whether it is true or not. What I do know is that it is difficult to use the truth for getting at the deepest structural fibres of one's spirit. Truth may not be the tool for it at all.

Not that I will tell lies. I have told many of course, but lying is a generous and honest act in a writer, something he was born to do and is therefore bound to continue as well as he is able in order to get as close to the truth as possible. Telling lies to explain the truth is where Art and Conscience meet uneasily.

Such a state is the other side of the coin to deception, like that island of such name in the South Atlantic which was thrown up by volcanic eruption and, being hollow inside, tricked ancient mariners into thinking it was larger and more important than it was, until they properly explored it and saw the true *lie* of the land, whereby it was confirmed that deception finally took in nobody, and that the island in any case was in continual eruption.

The older one gets the harder it becomes to lie with conviction. One's heart hardens, and one refuses to prevaricate either to entertain people or to save someone you love from pain. In other words, one will not compromise. One's integrity stiffens – though there is a danger of it becoming fossilised. The time when I could falsify with ease was a carefree golden age. I did not even have to think about it or make a decision to do so, but simply dissembled out of a positive joy of life. If I want to tell *lies* nowadays I have to start speaking the truth and wait for them to grow from that, though it makes little difference in the end.

Although it has become difficult to lie, self-interest prevents me telling enough truth to stop me living in the ease and comfort of creating fiction. And yet there is no danger, because I have been protected from speaking the truth. It hasn't occurred to me to try and tell it, and I haven't seen the need of it, nor felt it to be necessary. I thought I was already dealing with it, but realise that this is not so at all, because I didn't know that the truth about myself existed. It seemed that I lived the truth and breathed the truth as far as I myself was concerned.

Even in those years of sham, gullery, and make-believe I was searching for the truth. He who lies does so only because he feels he has more need of the truth than he who keeps silent, or than he who pompously professes to speak only the truth, which is next to saying nothing.

So let me pick up another strand of my raw material, and begin to interweave several threads as I go along.

5

Grandfather Burton hated dogs. He despised people who loved them and even those who showed them kindness.

He was blind in one eye, and that was the one he looked at animals with, unless they had hoofs or horns and might be tempted to go for him, in which case he fixed them with the other till he had stared them out and could afford to ignore them.

Dogs were as subservient and slavish as those who called them by name, petted and patted them. Such people were feminine and soft and did not know why they were on earth. They had to become friendly with dogs – as if dogs could ever tell them why or, more likely, inform them that it wasn't necessary to question why they were on earth. Because of these blind and sweeping prejudices a large section of English humanity was cut off from him, which may have been exactly how he wanted it, though I think he had little opinion about it either way. If he kept dogs it was only because they had their uses, but they got little thanks for it.

He was hard on human nature because it had him in its grip, though it must be said at the same time that he did not totally lack it. In my view there are neither good people nor bad people, no total devils or complete devilesses. It is impossible to give a person the face and soul of reality without first picking away the bad and showing it to whoever is interested. It must be put back later, however, otherwise the created picture will hang lop-sided and at some time crash down into splinters.

Women who were close to Burton disliked and feared him, as did those members of his own family. Yet women unacquainted with his true side – if there was such a thing – were attracted by a certain distance he put between them, and occasionally fell in love across the gap of it, a space which could be well seasoned by his wry and bawdy sense of humour when it wasn't filled by a dignified and possibly defensive silence.

In his prime and hey-day he was over six feet tall and extremely strong. There was no fat on him and not much muscle either, but he could twist an iron bar and shape steel, so that he might not have been as unfeeling as many people accused him of being. Nevertheless he was irascible and violent, and as rigid with others as he was rigorous with himself.

He was born in 1868, so perhaps this book is in some way a tardy monument to his centenary. What power he possessed came from the strength of his working arms, which enabled him to provide bread and shelter for his family when lack of such meant starvation or the workhouse. He swore that everyone but he was bone-idle, that they were, to use his favourite phrase, 'as soft as shit'. But while his wife and eight children were said to hate the sight of him he was respected by others as a first-class blacksmith, having won many prizes in Nottinghamshire and neighbouring counties.

There was a showcase of exhibition horseshoes in his kitchen, and I have one on my desk for a talismanic object while I write. Burton was said to have so steady a hand and eye that he could 'shoe Old Nick's nag so that all four hoofs would come clattering back out of bloody Hell itself'. Known in the trade as a careful worker, his forge was always neat and tidy. He was a man who had to know exactly where every hammer and plier was, something his own father might have instilled into him as a youth but which continually made tension when he applied such a rule to his house.

Burton governed the roost of a five-roomed cottage which was made up of a large communal kitchen, a parlour, and three bedrooms upstairs – one for the parents which contained an old four-poster curtain-drawn bed, one for the three sons, and one for the five girls, though it was rare for all the children to be at home together after they were grown up.

Outside there was a lot of ground for such a small house, with a garden at the back and enough space in front for pigs, chickens, and pigeons to be kept. Burton dug a good plot of vegetables, and every Friday night, after he came home from work on his tall bicycle, he dragged a great iron shit-bucket from the outhouse opposite the kitchen door and carried it to the end of the garden for manure. He had a gun and could shoot well, in spite of one eye being dead.

I took well to the long afternoons at Burton's house, enjoying the boredom in that it was a time when nobody troubled me. Out of such boredom came enlightenment, for what it was worth, because I'd press my nose to the chicken wire and watch the well-padded white cock with his waving red comb stalking around the compound and spitefully darting his beak at the others. Then he would go among the hens (some of whom were almost as big as he) and peck them cruelly out of the way even when they weren't bothering him – especially, it seemed, when they were minding their own business. I saw then that Burton was a like gaffer of the roost, who lorded it over his wife and daughters.

My memories have thrived on all else I've heard about him, but even his children are getting to be old men and women, and his grandchildren are middle-aged. Such distance might put truth on a pedestal, but truth is a dubious idol when made in the image of people who are either dead or far away. Each incident concerning him has more than one version, and so certain parts of this book are closer to a novel than others. Dealing with actualities, I see truth as riddled with the power of betrayal and broken with uncertainty. In such a dilemma time might be more reliable in that it reveals everything, even that which was never there, so that I end up with a bargain after all. And time also leaves everything behind. It has many uses. It cures a spiritual injury that treacherous truth inflicted, and drips such vital oil into the great machine of circumstance that nothing can be done without it.

But it doesn't change the opinions of Burton's children about what sort of a man he was. If he loved his children at all he only did so until they began to grow up and show what they were made of. If they revealed traits which came from the gentle subservience of the mother that was all right, but any that cropped up from him were put down with more than necessary harshness.

Burton was a tyrant but, as with all tyrants, the girls at least found ways of deceiving him. If one wanted to go out late in the evening to see a boy-friend she would throw her coat from the back bedroom window, then nip down through the front door as if on her way to the lavatory across the yard, treading quietly so that Burton, already in bed, would hear nothing. It was risky getting back into the house at midnight or after, but one of the other girls would respond to gravel thrown at the window and open the door if it had been locked in the meantime.

When Burton sent one of his daughters to buy fried fish for his supper she didn't return till eleven o'clock – having spent an hour with her boy-friend. Because she was so late he guessed what she had been up to, and in fact had only sent her out in order to confirm his suspicions. He gave her a good hiding and made sure she didn't go free at night for a few weeks – though her coat went flying from the back window several times before the ban was lifted. There were some uses, after all, in having a lavatory set apart from the house.

His daughters were ill-treated because he expected them to follow the same pattern he had forced on his wife, and he didn't know that times were changing. They fared badly because they rebelled, and they rebelled against Burton because the mother had not, and they saw where it had got her. By the time they reached twenty they had had enough of him, and they had enough of him in them not to put up with him a minute longer than they had to.

When Ivy came home one night at half past eleven Burton berated her for being the last in.

'Well,' she shouted back, 'somebody's got to be last in, ain't they?'

He gave her a vicious clout across the face and didn't speak to her for five years. The only recognition of her existence was that he would sometimes spit in her direction. She was thirty years old at the time.

Burton worked at Wollaton Pit after the Great War, and occasionally at the end of the day he would send word to his wife, by one of the colliers who passed Engine Town on his way home, that he would be working till three in the morning. Mary-Ann therefore made up some food and got one of the girls to take it. Whoever this job fell to would walk the two miles along lonely Wollaton Road and, afraid of being jumped on from the dark, she would carry a bag of pepper to throw in the face of any man who might try to molest her. When she got to the pit Burton looked at her with surprise and irritation. 'What the bloody hell are you doing here?'

'I've brought you some supper.'

He gave a grunt and said: 'You needn't have bothered.'

And she walked back with his sour greeting rankling so much that she didn't think once about the paper bag clutched in her hand. When she did, while opening the gate latch at home, it was only to wonder why she hadn't thrown it in his face for talking to her like that.

On a certain Sunday morning one of his daughters – I won't say who – was making his mustard before dinner. No one else was in the room but me. She shook the yellow powder out of the tin into a small basin, then poured in the requisite amount of water. I was very young, and sat on the floor by the table, and saw her spit – twice – into the mixture. Then she violently spun the fork around in the basin as if Burton's very soul was in it.

His three sons who also became qualified farriers, did no better in that Burton demanded the same standards from them that he had lived by himself, though setting them for his sons was one way of not having to follow them as thoroughly as others were expected to, since they were doing it for him.

They had to saw logs on the horse by the pigsty and chop them into sticks, fetch buckets of water with a yoke from the well up the slope behind the garden 300 yards away, as well as feed the pigs and clean out the sty. They didn't take well to this, though the only form of rebellion open to them was a stubborn idleness when orders fell too thick and fast.

On Sunday morning the brass candlesticks and ornaments were lifted from the fireplace shelf and, together with the horseshoes that were unhooked from inside the cabinet, spread over the table to be polished by Burton's two daughters still with the family. Cleaning the brasses and the table 'silver' was made into a ritual because it had to be done, and because nobody liked doing it. Ritual was easier than just plain work, and kept the house to a good standard for the family as well as Burton, though they would have felt happier doing it had he been less tyrannical.

All visible metal had to shine and look presentable for a blacksmith, to be appeased by polish and work. Whenever his married daughters visited the house he would not let them help in this, and neither could the men do it. It was a job solely for the unmarried girls.

Burton believed that, since he worked, everybody should work. He was the one who set me to labouring as a child, whereas my own father had not been able to succeed in it. It offended the sight of Burton's good eye to see even a child idle, so that from being a spectator of his own tasks in the garden I was soon hauling a barrow, weeding, digging, getting in coal, chopping wood, cleaning out pigeon coops, or darting down the lane on errands.

Work was a virtue, the only one. Even the straight way he stood when at rest proclaimed it. And while the better half of me agreed with him it must have been the other side that led me to become a writer.

Rather than write the truth I will work mindlessly in the garden or slump into a fit of sloth that lasts for days, or flee from it in the car as fast as the twisting lanes will allow.

And coming back to it, as one must, I will versify, falsify, elaborate, and boast, but be careful not to tell a significant lie in case someone should gloatingly inform me how near to the truth it is. For lies are as plain as footprints left on a beach still wet from the sucked-out tide. It is difficult to tell lies if one is facing the truth.

The fear that reaching some form of truth will reduce me to silence is an unbearable thought, but it would only shut my organ-box for a time, for after a while even the most stunning truth no longer shines or intimidates because of the familiarity it has meanwhile gained. One then denies it, and looks for it once more.

It is impossible to find. Vacillation is the blood of life. A mind made up is a dead mind. To decide is to act, and to act is to commit an injustice. To search for truth proves how fickle and disloyal one is, and untrustworthy to the earth. One is a member of the elect, in fact, a spiritual gypsy who must search for truth but be careful not to find it.

At the same time one wants to tell the truth in a single sweep of speech or pen, just as one longed of old to give out a big lie that would flatten all others by its weight and precision, a manoeuvre of the subconscious, perhaps, that might have landed one at the threshold of truth but never did.

The Big Lie consists of a million petty lies, and the Big Truth is made up of countless insignificant truths. All rules coalesce and ring true, and so are not to be trusted. Or maybe the Fat Complete Truth is merely a single unit of these myriad Big Truths, enlarged either by false brooding or grandiose boasting. The Big Lie can also be made out of innumerable small truths, and the most minute truth can grow from a million great lies.

There is no set law of moral divination, no comfort to be offered. Truth and lies do not exist. One may get nearer to truth by approaching it as if there were no such thing, while taking care not to get too close and therefore be dazzled by it. The impossible task is to remove the important coal-burning Truth from the million Big Truths that are so insignificant they are not worth considering. It is a question of continuing a fruitless search that might lead around regions of madness, or staying in the comfort of half-truths with which one has managed well enough so far. Defeat is the only final truth one ever gets, though a search for truth promises the most valuable defeat because it has most to teach.

Since everything is the truth, it becomes a matter of selection, and therefore distortion which, though it might be harmonious, gets to the antithesis of truth. But if there is no such thing as truth, one still has to search for it so as to prove it, and to know that one only hunts what does not exist, otherwise there would be no point in pursuing it. That which is plain before one's eyes needs no pursuing.

So it is tempting to believe that truth is fiction, yet fiction has nothing to do with the sort of truth I have in mind, since fiction is concerned with disguising the truth to such an extent that it becomes art, and is unrecognisable as the truth because it is even more powerful than the truth, depicting truth as something which it is not.

A frequently employed word soon loses its significance, and the word Truth does so more easily than most. The reality of truth, however, retains its meaning, though it is difficult to isolate and define such an illusive reality.

There are as many truths on earth as there are individuals, and there are as many truths in each individual as there are individuals on earth.

One of Burton's grown-up sons who went with him as a black-smith down the pit would receive an occasional hard thump if he seemed to be slacking on the job, or if some piece of work wasn't up to a good fit or a high polish.

Burton had no time for the waywardness or irresponsibility of youth, and made it appear, with much success, as if he had never had any himself. Maybe he was jealous of it, or bitter about the fact that he had already lost it.

Memory was not a function to which he gave free play, and so it seemed as if he had none, either for good things or bad. He never mentioned his parents or talked about the 'good old days'. Like sweat, speech was valuable. The pride of such illiterates often led them to ignore the meaning of what was said, not only between boss and man but also between equals. Burton would say something irrelevant in response to a statement, or merely nod, so as to let whoever made it know that he may or may not have taken it in, and that if by any chance he had he would understand it at his leisure. There would be time enough then to decide whether or not to reply. It was formal, high-minded, and mean.

Being literate myself, though connected to several who were not by close and recent ties (my father was never able to read or write), causes me to wonder what mark it has left in me, even if reduced by now to an idiosyncratic quirk which some-one on the same intellectual level might see as conceit or selfish-ness.

To move into the rich kingdoms of literacy in one genera-tion is more complicated than I could have thought when first beginning to read and write. What I consider to be my slow-ness of perception is perhaps an unconscious though deliberate ploy to retain some of the defensive and often advantageous traits of my antecedents. If some meaningful remark is made, either good for me or otherwise, I do not think at the moment I should get the full gist of it. A few minutes might go by before, having chewed it over like an Eskimo his piece of fat in the snow, I accept its full importance and decide to work up a suitable reply.

It would seem true of a man like Burton that literacy might not be a great advance. To gain such a thing he would not be prepared to pay the price of giving up a certain central feeling of quality and aloneness. To recover from pneumonia after refusing an inoculation that promised to save you from what was said to be certain death might feel like victory indeed. And to live all one's life without being able to read or write in a world that shouted how damned you were for not having these gifts must have given one an untouchable sensation of great value.

At the same time Burton, being a qualified and talented blacksmith, realised his lack of education. Because of it he never felt able to join a society or a union, or any other organisation. He knew that something was missing and yet, because of his obdurate character, there was nothing he could do about it.

To learn reading and writing would mean relying on memory instead of instinct and second nature, and perhaps there were things in Burton's life that he did not want memory to get at, and one of them could have been his youth, which might have led him back to childhood. And what he would have found there none of us could say.

Perhaps he really had forgotten his younger days by the time he reached forty. He felt older to his sons than their friends' fathers looked, though he was the same age. But he was less approachable in a human and fatherly manner, and if Burton did remember his youth it was only so that he could put the experience of it to such good use that his children stood little chance of enjoying their own in his presence.

Everyone agreed that his cunning was formidable. He was once walking into town with a man who was said to be deaf, though Burton didn't believe it. When he let a half-crown slip from his pocket the man turned abruptly at the noise. Burton picked it up, put it back, and went on without mentioning it.

But cunning never goes by itself. There is always cruelty

23

wrapped up in it somewhere. Often after work and as a way of earning extra money Burton would go to Wollaton Park to ring bulls and pigs, jobs which few could do unless they had prodigious strength. Yet even strong men shunned such work because it was regarded as one of the cruellest trades, though Burton was said not to mind it because he took delight in being cruel.

Since he never talked about his own father no one had an inkling of what he'd been like. He died before my mother was born, so she couldn't tell anything. Perhaps he was more humane than Burton, who might have modelled himself on one of his grandfathers. But if this was so I shall never know who it was, for if your spade tries to dig too deep it only swings freely in the air so that both Time and Truth draw back.

But I did hear, much later, that in fact Burton had two brothers and two sisters, and that one of his brothers was called George Burton, who kept a blacksmith's workshop at Carlton, and had at one time lived in Wales. But Burton never mentioned them, or had anything to do with them, and no one was ever able to say what his reasons were. It might have been those brothers and sisters who cut *him* off, and if this was so it seemed unnecessary for his family to wonder why.

When Burton wasn't present his sons and daughters always referred to him by surname, never 'Father' or 'Ernest' – as if he were a fierce stranger who had been put in charge of them by some malevolent authority. It is possible that he did not model himself on anyone in particular, but simply emerged from the knotted roots of his past, and was finished off by his own self-centred inviolable opinion of himself, as in any person of strength, or of certain hidden weaknesses.

Unlike many men of the present century he had never been in the Army. He abominated such an institution and thought that anyone who joined or allowed himself to be ensnared into it was even lower than a dog. He did not feel threatened by foreign power or alien system, and he would not have protected any government which felt itself in peril or which told him that his own safety was at risk. He owned no property and lived by his labour and skill, so saw little connection between the government and the people. When his eldest son Oliver

24

enlisted during the Great War he only forgave him because he was killed, for even Burton was not so hard of soul that he could hate the dead.

Until quite late in life he never worked for a boss, having been trained as a blacksmith by his father, so that he inherited the forge at Lenton. This was situated on a lane running beside the railway from Derby Road to Old Church Street. I remember passing it as a child, by which time Burton had given it up for lack of customers and gone to work at Wollaton Pit. Though the motor car came in during his lifetime I never heard him complain that it had ruined his trade.

I walked by the forge with my sister when we were children, on one of our long treks to the shores of the Trent in summer. The locked-up building seemed no more than a shed and looked as if it would soon fall down, though someone had put a strong lock on the rotten door to make sure no vandals went in and helped it to collapse over them.

8

When my nine-year-old son becomes ill, or hurts himself in any way, I am pitched into a turmoil of mental agony. I am the one who put him to whatever pain he might suffer during his time on earth.

To cause someone to be born is to send them alone into the dark. Thus the most excruciating guilt comes with having given life to a child. The remorse of treachery, or the biting pain of having been betrayed, is nothing compared to this. A child can claim to have been betrayed by the biological forces of evolution if someone is cruel to him. The facts of life are no excuse for the infliction of injury or insult.

These thoughts are hard to bear, yet every truth begets its opposite. He is not my son, I tell myself. As he grows older he is my friend and pupil. Beside the terrible fact that I presented

25

him with the certainty of death is the wonderful and undeniable truth that I caused him to have life. I have given him everything, just as I received everything, though even by making these self-evident remarks I seem to be robbing him of the richness of his existence. Whatever I do for him, he owes me nothing.

At the moment he trusts me as no one else can. The better world I hope to see on earth will not come in time to make his life secure. It is no secret that what I would like for him is only what I desire for myself. I want him to inherit paradise, just as I would like all others to inhabit it. Since this is impossible, the next best thing is to hope that he will strive as I do to create it for everybody, to construct it in himself as an example for others. That is the only way open, and since I often hesitate to touch it, how can I hope that he will do better?

Why is it that any giving of the truth turns my guts to coal and pitch? It paints a patch on my lung, blows my heart to pieces. I hate the truth. I do not feel righteous or happy when I think of searching for it. Whatever scraps I drag out, however many gems I get to, only make me feel more defeated than when, paddling along in neither truth nor falsehood, I at least lived in the easy half-light of enjoyment.

It leads me to question whether or not truth is my enemy, who beckons now and again but only to strike when I go towards him and get too close. Is it necessary to wallow in oblivion if one wants to keep even that little shred of happiness which one occasionally seems content with?

Don't touch the truth. Don't strive for it. Let it fester helplessly at the dim limits of the consciousness. The truth ruins itself if it is left alone. It becomes harmless. It eats itself to death if you don't search for it. Even lies vanish, I tell myself, knowing that they do not.

It is an admission of defeat to turn towards the lit-up city of Great Truth and hope for anything beneficial from it. If up to now one has been formed by the continual accretion of slapdash falsehood and social indoctrination that has been built upon the inherited factors of oneself, what hope is there of crawling out from it at this late hour?

At the end of the lane on which Burton's forge once stood was a field-gun from the horse-artillery, set on a concrete exhibition platform beyond some railings and surrounded by beds of flowers. This satanic memo from the Great War that had finished twenty years before was placed in front of some almshouses erected for the widows of heroes whom the world was fit for, but who perished in the war to end wars. It was the badge of what had warped the women's lives, and they could dwell on that machine from their bedroom or parlour windows, and maybe reflect that it was a similar gun on the German side that had blown up their husbands.

Artillery was the most efficient killer of the Great War, according to the mad and fascinating statistics of the official histories. While forty per cent of the casualties were caused by bullets, sixty per cent of the men were killed or mangled by shellfire. The gun I stared at as a child turned the air raw, and I could never resist pressing my face against the cold railings and gazing for a long time at its grisly and intricate mechanisms.

But I did not see a woman looking from a window of the building itself, nor going into any of the doors. The place always seemed decorously deserted. On Armistice Day the gun would be surrounded by wreaths of Flanders poppies made by the crippled in their factories and workshops. I believe that during the Second World War the gun was hauled off for scrap, or taken away in case German parachutists should drop from the sky and start to use it on the shabby landscape round about.

Burton's daughter Edith married a gunner in the Great War, and he was killed after leaving her with one child. But she didn't live at the almshouses because she then married another gunner who unfortunately survived the war – because no man could have been worse to her. The savagery that he brought home from the mud of the Ypres Salient (but which no doubt had been fed on much that was there before) was execrated even by Burton, who was respectable and civilised by comparison.

The man's name was also Ernest, but he was known to everyone as 'Blonk', a mysterious label put on him by his childhood friends from Radford Woodhouse, which lasted him till the day of his death. But Blonk, I discovered later, was a North Country word meaning sullen, fitting him well as a sobriquet, because he was a demon with boots and fists, and he used both on his wife, together with the blackest language his brain could muster.

He worked alternately as a bricklayer's labourer and a coal-miner, changing jobs as the mood took him and indulging his passion for playing football whenever a spell of unemployment came between. The expression on his face was tough and cunning, and he had a head of springy and grizzled hair, his whole bearing an image of impacted strength. When Burton told Edith, just before she married Blonk, that he was no good and would be sure to lead her a dance, she naturally thought he was trying to keep her under his thumb as he had always done, and so ignored his warning.

Wayward Edith had already been a few years in service, and wouldn't listen to her father. In fact the three of Burton's girls who married young were wayward, and were not made so entirely by his bullying. It is said that such girls do not marry well – whatever that may mean. They are never satisfied, being too mettlesome either to get a good husband, or to be content with a bad one. Perhaps they deserved neither, and should not have married at all. They did because many men found that flighty trio of blacksmith's daughters attractive, and sooner or later they succumbed to wedlock in order to get out of Burton's clutches.

A hard time was had by husbands and wives alike, some of it due to the era they lived in, though all three women are now alive, while their husbands are dead. Yet Edith, who was one of the best, was said to have got the worst.

Burton's inevitable confrontation with Blonk ended in Edith and her eight children being more or less cut off from her parents. It was a ban that Burton put on the husband more than his daughter, for whenever better-off members of the family from Leeds or St Neots heard of her plight and brought clothes for the children, he always saw that she got them.

And he did occasionally have a kind word when he met her children in the fields around Engine Town. His wife would never turn them empty-handed from the door, though they were often afraid to go there for fear of meeting Burton, who could be fiercesomely harsh if he was in a bad mood.

Edith was his favourite daughter, being the most high-spirited and independent in getting away from him sooner than any of the others. She was tall, with reddish hair and blue eyes, and a well-formed body. Throughout my childhood she had a great knack of organising food for her children, and whenever I was near her house at mealtimes, which was often, there was always the chance of getting some. She never complained at seeing me queue up with the rest, though there was little enough to go round.

Why she appeared more profoundly connected to me than anyone else in my family I don't know, but when I was some weeks old a malfunctioning of the heart got me in its grip which turned my face and body blue so that I appeared to be at the point of death. My mother was also ill, and March did not go out like a lamb that year, because snow was drifting down and lay thick everywhere. Edith wrapped me in a shawl, put on her coat, and set off with me across the quarter-mile stretch of the park to the doctor's place beyond. She told me a long time afterwards that there was no knowing whether I would be dead or alive when the shawl was opened in his surgery.

A few years later she and my mother got hold of tickets for an organ recital at the Albert Hall in Nottingham. They took me with them, saying we were going to hear some thunder and lightning. We stayed half an hour at the concert, and then withdrew from my first experience of listening to Bach.

Truth menaces the soul, and to turn to it for illumination will only increase its monolithic power. Having done long enough without it, and not lived totally in the night of my own falsehoods, I don't need help from it now. Nor does it crave any assistance from me. The truth ignores those who do not recognise defeat. It can only help those who are able to do without it – though they may still yearn for its support to keep them on the switchback motorway through life.

Truth is the novelist's enemy. If I steer a positive course towards it I forfeit the greater use of inspiration. To decide for one or the other is to make the best of a bad job, but a writer who seeks truth betrays his talent, abandoning the divine for a mundane quality that deadens intuitive power, and ruins his conjuring tricks. He accepts morality but relinquishes his soul. Everything has its price.

Yet one occasionally employs truth in order to cement and solidify chaotic constructions. Everything has its uses, also. Without some concept of truth one would be unable to say yes or no, and it is necessary to say yes or no in order to make decisions, without which power one cannot be free. But to speak the truth so as to say everything in a single sentence is an impossibility.

If God manifested Himself, claiming to be the Truth, He would be quickly disowned. God is life, perhaps, but not the Truth. As soon as one claims to speak the truth one becomes a politician, or a historian, or a bully, or a bore, or all of them put together – but certainly not a novelist. Refusing to speak the truth (being unable to do so), one is thrown back on the imagination, on uncertainty and exploration. One becomes picturesque in spirit, and not to be relied upon, and condemned to die a slow life.

The wish to create a single sentence of universal wisdom or truth is laudable, but such an achievement, even if it were possible, would leave one heartless and without blood, a dry skin of emptiness, all but dead and frozen in the mind, while at the same time seeming to be most alive at having spoken what one imagined to be the truth.

There are those who have in their hearts a simple truth, some political mountain or emotional fact, but it is nearly always another's truth which they try and live by, or several truths drawn together into a few drab maxims of equal falsehood which they try to make everybody else believe in. If it were their own truth they would not be so happy, or so totally dedicated. They who live by the word shall perish by the word. Life exposes you to death, but Truth rots the spirit.

An artist cannot formulate the one truth, any more than he can live by one truth. The only truth he can cling to is that there are no lies. Every sentence that comes to him is the truth, no matter how weird or contradictory, how sacred or antithetical to all human values, or even how true it appears to be. One can live without believing in anything, but only so as to respect everything.

This is a single truth out of millions. A writer who finds it necessary to construct some edifice around himself can only rely on inspired natural selection, sorting out those innumerable truths that he cannot otherwise control.

One drills deep into the mind in search of some truth with which to intensify life, driving down through soil and subsequent rock so that right from the start hard resistance flies to the drill as if to pulverise its power and break it to pieces. One must go where the rock is hardest, cut into it with the utmost power of concentrated thought and recollection. If the drill doesn't break, one isn't even trying.

Truth does not come from wanting it. And as a phantom it melts away when I try to take hold. Sometimes it comes unasked if I think on nothing. At the same time there are truths about myself that might never be revealed in this or any other way, and it is necessary to realise that truth can also play one false, concealing secrets never to be obtained by leaving truth alone.

All this is to say that I do not know, and by admitting it I build up more confidence in myself and feel further advanced

31

by time and spirit than if I definitely and positively swore by all the fixed stars that I knew, and put forth an opinion that I defied anyone to gainsay.

The first step in the search for truth is *not to know*, to accept the dilemma of uncertainty rather than bite the sour truth of polluted bread.

II

Burton voted from time to time in General Elections. In the 1890s he 'supported' the successful Liberal candidate for the West Nottingham constituency, a Mr J. Yoxall, who stood on a platform of House of Lords reform, rural education, and industrial insurance. Later in life Burton voted Labour. Much to his chagrin his wife Mary-Ann voted Conservative and they had many loud arguments about it, though this was one issue over which he couldn't finally have his own way, no matter how jeeringly he went on, which was probably why Mary-Ann persisted in it.

He did not believe that politics could have much effect on his existence. It was as if he had been born before the age of politics, knowing in his deeper self that they could alter nothing, though somewhere wanting to believe that they could. While there were horses in the world, used as the prime force of haulage, he was his own master, and no system could change that. At least it did not for most of his life.

He was never patriotic, and seeing me once with a Union Jack flag that had been given out at school for some jubilee or other, he told me sharply to 'hurl the bloody thing away.' He was too proud and sure of himself, too skilled in his work to get hooked by any concept of job-lot nationalism. You were soft in the head and the backbone if you were for Queen and country, or for King and country. To believe in that sort of thing was a sure form of bum-sucking. You'd got no guts. You

32

were frightened of the dark. As a man you had your work and your family – though you may well like one and not the other. But the country you lived in, in the form of its government, was always threatening both with destruction, so he did not see how anyone could be wet-eyed about it.

Being a man with few friends, everybody in the district knew him. It wasn't as if they were afraid of him, or distrusted him exactly, but he was recognised as the smith, the man apart, a person with secrets they could never share. It was as if he had come to the country hundreds of years ago, and then forgotten he had done so, and where it was he had come from, but that look in his eyes as he gazed at the woods in the distance was as empty and far-seeing as if some part of him did after all remember that he had undergone a tremendous and difficult migration. He worked much and talked little, so perhaps that accounted for him having more acquaintances than friends.

The only foreigners he knew were a couple of Belgian refugees billeted on them during the Great War, and his one observation was that they were a 'rum pair' – though he never said as much to their faces. His wife Mary-Ann remarked that they had to have chocolate to drink instead of tea, which seemed extremely strange to her.

Burton had no belief in God. And after death it was the end, nothing, a disaster you went to sleep under before it hit you, if you were lucky. Nevertheless, his children were packed off to Sunday School for nearly ten years of their lives, the result of which was a glass-fronted case of books in the parlour recess, sober volumes they had brought home as prizes, and the first such collection I'd seen in a private house. From time to time Mary-Ann would give me one to take home and keep.

Burton only bundled the kids off to bible class so as to get the house clear and make free with his wife without too many inquisitive ears wondering what they were up to and what those noises were. If the Sunday Schools of England in all their Godly work did not produce a nation of Christians they at least helped, when living-space was intolerably cramped, to keep a bit of private love-life on the go. One wonders if those sanctimonious men and women really knew what they were up to, or whether they didn't just look upon Sunday School teaching as a sure way of keeping themselves out of mischief.

Even in their sixties Burton and Mary-Ann, when I used to stay there, went upstairs on Sunday afternoon 'for a bit of a sleep' as they put it. Burton tried to get me off to Sunday School with the Ollington children who lived in a cottage on the edge of Robins Wood, across the Cherry Orchard, but I came out with the statement that I did not believe in God, a straight answer which amused him so much that he winked at Mary-Ann, laughed loudly, and didn't mention it again.

He either recognised me in him, or gave in to the unknown part of me stemming from my father, whom he implacably disliked – though he never said so. Rather than face the truth he preferred to keep silent, and thereby enrich himself in the only way possible.

12

To define the hidden truth is to change life for the better. One becomes more aware and more alive when it is no longer concealed, and a truth that reveals other hidden truths expands the limits of consciousness in such a way that it would seem one was hardly born before that first truth became apparent.

The greatest truth of all would be to control the visionary light that flares in the mind for a split second at the point of dying, but which is put out for ever by death – and so is denied to us. I ask too much. Burton, who was strong in other things, was unfortunate enough not to realise that such questions existed. In one sense he was too strong to think they were necessary. Where illiterates ignore many things, literates question them so as to bask in the comfort of ignorance when they get no answer.

To want truth is the beginning of defeat. To distrust truth is the first step to paradise. Life ends where truth begins. The search for truth is a momentary aberration that will not last, though a person should not refuse any experience that clamours to mind, for it may be a lock on the canal of life, carrying him to a higher level of consciousness.

Paradise, desired by everyone, is a place where neither truth nor lies exist, and where all is provided. But paradise can never be real, though the desire for it is. The truth this leads to is unimportant in that sense. But I am different from Burton, able to believe that an answer of yes or no to such a question may produce the first truth that will open the door to this search, or make me so despair of it that I will give up and go on in the darkness as before. People who cannot make decisions are in the hands of destiny. Those who do not ask questions are in their own hands.

Life, like art, is the only way of approaching the truth. An artist can never say that art is not enough, though he may often be tempted to. If one were not tempted one would have to admit that the breath of truth had passed one by, in which case one would not even reach that zone of chaos in which everything might be understood. The first chapter of Genesis is a perfect description of the creative process.

When I see a possibility of happiness coming to me I will not help to make it real, out of a fear that if I succeed I shall no longer have the moral stamina and rectitude to know that I am incapable of speaking the truth.

Yet if I accepted the happiness that waits for me it would then cease to be the happiness I now imagined it would be, and I would still be armed and plagued with the necessity of searching for the truth.

One must continually strive for happiness, because the unhappiness that comes with it will always be more fruitful than the unhappiness of non-endeavour one left behind.

Paradise is a long way off. I try to get at the truth, as if to do so may bring a certain amount of happiness. At the same time I find myself utterly distrusting it. Sooner or later one must make up one's mind.

I was treated well by Burton because, apart from being able and willing to labour physically, I also bothered myself industriously with books and writing paper.

I sat on a chair in the kitchen, by the light of an oil lamp shining from a hook above the table, reading or drawing maps, and I know that he looked at me strongly now and again because he had not seen the like of it before. Sometimes he passed the newspaper and asked me to recite the latest news from Abyssinia, where 'that swine Mussolini was knocking people about'.

When I walked in on Sunday afternoon after playing in the garden or along the lane outside, Mary-Ann and Emily would already be laying the tea-table and waiting for that peculiar authoritative stamp of Burton as he came downstairs in his stockinged feet.

If he saw the cat in front of the fire he would kick it clear – though it was often alert and leapt out of sight before he came into the room. If the dog stayed there, being near enough human to hope for better things, he would usually move that away also.

But if he was in an affectionate mood he would grip the dog around its long mouth and hold the jaws fast, an action which, as well as being painful, induced in the poor animal a feeling of claustrophobia and panic, so that it struggled to get free, much to Burton's delight and the loud protests of his wife and daughters. It whined and wriggled until he let it go with as friendly a pat as he could muster under the thwarting circumstances, a gesture which was the nearest I saw him get to an expression of guilt.

And so he came in for his tea, having taken care to re-establish his reputation in front of the family so that normal life could be resumed once more. There would be salmon and cucumber and jam-pasty to eat, a combined smell of fish and vinegar and new-baked dough which was enough to make anyone's mouth water. But he never had much of it, not being a big eater, in spite of his work. He would pull on his boots and go into the yard or garden to busy himself for an hour before walking off for an evening bout at some pub or other.

He lived close to Nottingham, a lifetime spent within a few miles of the Goose Fair and Market Place. Born and bred, married and buried at Lenton, he was to live ten years at Bridge Yard, and later for many more at a block of three cottages on Lord Middleton's land that were shown by the Ordnance Survey maps of the late nineteenth century as 'Old Engine Houses', though they were always known locally as Engine Town. Demolished in 1939, a few months after watertaps and electricity had been put in, they made way for the spread of bungalows from Nottingham.

The cottages were connected by a motorable high-hedged sunken lane to Radford Woodhouse – a compact settlement of three streets – beyond which one went by paved road to the city. But to other localities there were only tracks across the fields. To reach Aspley or Basford one went up 'Colliers' Pad', a leafy and narrow bridle-path that ran by an open space of undulating scrubland known as the Cherry Orchard, a way that was often used by miners going home from Radford or Wollaton Pits.

Burton never thought of himself as an urban man, even when his house was on the actual city limits and he could find himself in Nottingham – so to speak – simply by walking to the end of the yard. There were still many fields to cross before coming to the packed houses of Old Radford and the first lively outlying pubs of the city. He watched them from behind the fence, as if daring them to come up and get him.

He couldn't be doing nothing for long, however, and before going back to what work there was he ceased his gazing and suddenly, to spite the lane a few yards away as well as shock it, he gobbed into the middle, and then turned his back on it.

This gesture was characteristic, a spit at the bars of the fire to hear it sizzle, or down into the lane to pay it out for never moving. The fire was unbeatable as far as his saliva was concerned, but the lane couldn't answer back. There was no contempt in his spitting. It was just an eternal testing of the forces of nature to make sure they were always as he expected them to be. Satisfied that they were, he could then return to his work.

Burton, in the great words of Ecclesiasticus, was the smith, 'sitting by the anvil, and considering the iron work, the vapour of the fire wasteth his flesh, and he fighteth with the heat of the furnace: the noise of the hammer and anvil is ever in his ears, and his eyes still look upon the pattern of the thing that he maketh; he setteth his mind to finish his work, and watcheth to polish it perfectly.' He trusted to his hands, and was wise in his work.

But on Saturday night he donned his best suit. In fact he had two, which seemed an unparalleled luxury compared to the state of my own father at the time. There was a black one and a brown one – with boots to match each, of the sort that laced high and covered the ankles. Their good-quality leather glistened from the shine I had just given them as, in the chosen pair, he made his way down the dry or muddy lane, according to season, and on under the long tunnel-like railway bridge whose darkness at six o'clock on gloomy winter mornings had so much frightened my mother on her way to the lace factory in Nottingham where she worked from the age of fourteen.

Burton would stop at the beer-off in Radford Woodhouse for his first pint, then go on by the disused lime kilns up to Wollaton Road. His son Oswald lived in a cottage near the junction, and he would call in to see if everything was all right, then continue the two-mile walk into Nottingham. In his own world he was without fear, and he despised anyone who was not the same, though he would occasionally condescend to talk to them for reasons of work or business. Those who were similar in stature might be lucky to get a passing nod from time to time, for he was exceedingly conscious of his height, and held himself accordingly.

As a child I once caught a glimpse of him at the saloon bar when someone going in opened the pub door. Burton was standing up, talking to other men, the upper half of his tankard arm held well into his side, the beer pot straight at his mouth when he drank, though the stance and picture was by no means a stiff one. Then I dodged out of sight in case he should see me.

At Sunday dinner a quart bottle would be set on the table, which only he was allowed to drink. If his grown-up sons wanted to take beer at the same meal they had to go and buy a pint of their own, though they could only bring a glass to the table, never the actual bottle. If they did there would be ructions which would end in them getting knocked down if they didn't take it away.

He'd send me out on Sunday morning to the Woodhouse for his ale, and I remember the smell of it as the handsome but hurried young woman at the beer-off poured it into the white enamel funnel she held over the bottle. He once rewarded me with a glass when I got back, though I should have known there was some trick in it, for he was delighted when I staggered away from the meal half drunk. On another occasion he tempted me to a pinch of snuff, which set me sneezing around the house and yard for hours.

I was one of the few who appreciated his sense of humour, for he was universally known among his family as a 'rotten old swine', mostly because all his actions added up to the fact that he liked making people dance to his tune.

14

Vindictive parasitic thorn-bushes tangle with free-growing evergreens along two sides of the garden. Physical work relieves the pressure. I still occasionally take a leaf out of Burton's book.

Using a short thin-bladed Swedish handsaw to cut through the trunks close to the soil I then (wearing gloves) grip each spiked creeper in turn and pull with all my strength so that its dozen long tentacles slowly ungrasp from the bushes and trees

39

round about. I spend much of the day at this, making a huge pyre of disentangled briars ready for burning in the morning.

The creepers are no longer strangling the veins and sinews of the bushes, so the greenery will grow more resplendently when spring fully comes. In this work I had no difficulty knowing that the brambles had to be separated from the bushes, and that the bushes were the only kind of truth I wanted to see.

Yet the creepers also had an existence. They choked and fed off the trees, and their small triangular thorns fetched blood when they scraped my wrist or ran in through a hole in the glove. They too have a tenacious life that has to be dragged out, but because most of the roots are left they will grow and spread everywhere again. The truth of the trees and bushes would not be complete without them.

Such reality cannot be perceived without struggle or blood being spilled. The heart must be bruised before truth comes out. How else can one find it? When the long thorn-covered tendrils were tugged from the bushes, leaves flew off and twigs snapped. If truth is to have any significance it can only be as a blood-brother.

Yet when his quest for truth begins to be answered, and these verities are made known after effort and illumination, I give in to the temptation to say they are lies, and find an excuse to disown them.

They create too much uncertainty, telling me they are not the truth because there are so many million truths, and that my judgement may have been at fault in picking the wrong ones. Every man has to make his own choices, not wait on God to do it. And if I think I have selected wrongly, the truths thus isolated must be lies. All one can believe in is the falsity of truth, and start again.

But fake truth carries the sheen of hope and optimism – like a counterfeit light before the dawn out of which the real day is bound to grow. A sham truth brings exhilaration, because even though I have decided that it is not the real truth, and have discarded it, at least I can persuade myself that I am getting closer to acceptable veracity.

The first failure is always the surest sign that I will find what

40

I want, I tell myself, swallowing the light so as not to vomit. In my lit-up state I curse the truth I was so ardently seeking before the blaze of its falsity struck me, before I was lured from the real path that was not solid enough to support the truth but where I was secure in the right of my own heart. Truth is a machine that turns the heart into a computer on which anyone can play a tune.

This halfway incandescence of the spirit is a safeguard. It can only be my downfall if I go beyond it. Yet if I do outdistance it I must keep possession of my own live backbone, because as a writer it is my vocation, for the benefit of myself and others, to bypass this self-evident falsity of truth and find out what exactitudes might exist in the furthest wilderness.

The greatest intoxication comes when I realise that there is no downfall. Such a possibility does not exist. I never go down. I do not fall. I can die, shrivel up, perish, rave in anguish at the soil and the sky. But I do not fall. This is so evident a truth that I accept it and know it to be true without any conditions whatsoever. It provides a sense of power and confidence, as well as a desperate strength to go in face of all disappointments and disasters.

An artist who sees that the falsity of truth is nothing better than a trap must sooner or later decide what it is he wants. If truth is not everything to him, it must be nothing, but if truth is nothing, then what is fit to take its place?

15

Burton was to regret the hard times he'd given Oliver, his eldest son.

As a youth, Oliver was led the fiercest dance of all, 'got kicked from pillar to post' because he had the misfortune to be Burton's firstborn and prime competitor. After one terrible bout he walked out and took a job as a blacksmith at Browns'

Sawmills near Wollaton, and none of the family knew where he slept, for he had no money to get lodgings.

His mother managed to send some dinner every day by one of his sisters – each time with a message imploring him to come home and make it up with his father. Burton had already grudgingly agreed to it, because if there was one thing worse than having an argumentative son in the house, it was having him away from it so that he could no longer be got at.

After a week Oliver relented, preferring to share a bed with his brothers than sleep on the newly seasoned planks in one of the Sawmill lofts. But he kept his job there.

A year or so later he started courting, but when his girl-friend came to call for him one day, Burton, in his forty-seventh year, took a fancy to her. She appears to have fallen for him, being a loose and saucy Radford tart, and the iron peace of the family was shattered. Burton went off with her for a few days to some place in Derbyshire. Oliver, who had been in love with the girl and was now in despair at everyone's perfidy, enlisted with the army as a blacksmith, for the Great War had begun.

So at forty-eight years of age Burton received news of his eldest son, and accounts differ as to how it came. One says that a white-faced twelve-year-old daughter went to the forge with the black tidings. How did he take it? He was shoeing a horse and, stunned by her own emptiness after the words of the telegram, she was afraid to interrupt his work, imagining it was more important to them and the world than what she had been fetched out of school to tell.

Her mother was at home, crying one minute, stunned and silent the next, clinging to the flickering light of disbelief whenever she had the strength – while blinds at the house had already been drawn.

Burton had seen her, and wondered why she was out of school, for he had insisted that none of his children should miss a minute of it. She couldn't tell whether he scowled especially at her, or whether he was niggled by the horse being unable to hold still, an animal that could sense before any of them the awful news in the air.

He hammered in the last four nails of the shoe, and even then

42

she did not dare shout what she had come to tell, because three or four other people were standing around. She had thought on her way there to go up and whisper it, but was more afraid of that than doing it any other way. When the horse was pushed unwillingly backwards between the cart-shafts she called out: 'Oliver's dead, our dad.'

'What did you say?'

He stopped in picking up his tools, but heard the first time, and his question was only a means of keeping himself steady, and the preparation for him to stand bolt-still for a few seconds in the silence created by the information among the men waiting around, and for him to say in a sharp voice that astonished them all, and made them realise how terrible the by now not unusual news would be: 'I bloody well knew it!'

Oliver had not been killed at the Battle of the Aisne, or in the senseless slaughter at Loos, but on a moor in Norfolk. Some of his boisterous soldier-mates had, by way of a joke, fed rum to a string of mules he was to lead across the moor at dusk. Enlivened too much, they kicked him to death, and he wasn't found till the middle of the following day.

Another account, and probably the right one, says that he and his pals were taking a drink outside a pub near Hungerford in Berkshire. It was a bitter-cold day in the middle of November and they needed something to warm them. One soldier dared a maid to feed whisky to one of their horses and, being gentle and persuasive, she managed to do it.

The animal ran wild, galloping around the yard with such energy that it seemed they would never get it back to barracks. Oliver tried some tackling, and was killed by a blow at the head from one of its hooves. The horse had to be shot, and the girl who had given it whisky got into great trouble for her mindless action.

All nine of the Burtons were sitting at Sunday dinner, a large joint of meat about to be carved. A knock sounded at the door, and Mary-Ann came back with a telegram saying that Oliver had been killed.

His body, clothed as the soldier he had been, was brought to them in a coffin which lay open for a day in the living-room. The children stood around, though some of the girls dared not at first come down from the bedroom to look. Burton made them, and gave orders that none of them was to cry. 'Anybody starts blubbering,' he said, the bones standing out from his unnaturally white face, 'and I'll kick 'em from arse-hole to breakfast time. There'll be no bleddy blawting in this family.'

He made such impossible demands, sometimes only to hear the sound of his own voice, and when they objected he was then committed to getting obedience, even though it might not matter to him whether he was obeyed or not. If only they had let him speak, and not cringed before every word, he might have had something to thank them for.

And they tried not to cry as they surrounded Oliver's coffin and looked at his twenty-two-year-old face. He was that rare youth who was liked by all his sisters, as well as loved by them. In spite of everything, he was also Burton's favourite son, and Burton knew he'd never been liked by him, though Burton had thought that one day Oliver would make as good a black-smith as himself.

There was a strange, chemical smell in the room. Two neighbours had come quietly in, and now the door burst open, and Florrie Voce from next door pushed through them and looked into the coffin. Her round flat Radford face suddenly bunched like a withered apple. 'What the bloody hell does *she* want?' Burton thought, and from her came a loud screaming of agonised distress which filled the whole house as if to split all the walls.

The effect was to tear into the children's hearts so directly that they too began to weep and wail, as if Oliver was finally getting his rightful dues. Mary-Ann resumed the quiet sobbing that had stricken her ever since hearing the news, and finally Burton himself – as they all witnessed – 'cried like a baby', his soul torn out of him at last.

The coffin was taken to Lenton cemetery on a gun-carriage, where Oliver was buried with full military honours to the tune of The Last Post. Fourteen riflemen fired a volley over his grave. It was a dull afternoon, laden with rain, and the echo of the shots soon died away.

When he could bear to talk about it Burton said to Mary-Ann that if he'd been with Oliver on that day, the bloody horse wouldn't have kicked him to death. He had a few tricks by which to tame it or keep it off. He slept with the vision of saving his son from all harm at its vicious antics, only to wake in the morning and face the further reality of his death. He was eventually buried next to him in the same churchyard.

As a child I used to go with my aunts to put flowers on Oliver's grave. They did so every week, even twenty or thirty years after he had died. The last time Burton went out of the house as an old man of nearly eighty, before his first and last illness which brought on death too suddenly for him to beat it or have much say in the matter, was to visit Oliver's grave and set flowers by it. Unlike his wife and daughters he would never put them in a vase of water, but merely lay them on the grave itself, stay a moment or two, grunt, and walk away.

On Thursday July 18th in the year 1974 of the Common (or Christian) Era – or 5734 years from the creation of the world by the Jewish calendar – I went to Nottingham to leave my adopted daughter there for a few days' holiday. It was a warm yet windy morning, a time for visiting graves, so first we went to the high and open cemetery at Bulwell, to that of her mother and my sister who had died of cancer at forty-two.

Like feckless people we had come without flowers, so took one from each of the surrounding tombs and got a posy up, laid it there where she was buried with my father, who also died of cancer at fifty-six.

All their lives they were torn at by anxiety, guilt, work, inexpressible terrors, or various combinations of these factors that gave them little happiness. Life is meagre with some people. It is like a small shark inside that will not let them rest. Their anxiety as a result of this continual gnawing turns them into victims as soon as they meet someone whom they think will ease their lives. Those who fear, but don't know why, are unable because of it to express the fears that torment them. It is the life-long deadlock of a small circle around which the shark of cancer swims and swims, waiting to bite. They are locked so securely in their own prison that freedom means nothing to them. And if they think of freedom from time to time it only locks them more firmly in it. They had their moments, as the saying goes, yet by and large they didn't find anywhere in the whole wide world to rest except under the earth when dead — near where my feet were standing.

In the afternoon we took my mother to Lenton Church to find her brother Oliver's grave. I'd been before but couldn't see it because the cemetery was in an indescribable condition: overgrown, neglected, almost abandoned, the blackened church now lost in a forgotten area, since most of the houses of the ancient district roundabout had been bulldozed into oblivion.

I don't think she'd been there for ten or twenty years, but we pulled up heaps of damp tangled sooty grass and finally got to it:

In loving memory of
Oliver
The beloved son of
Mary Ann and Ernest Burton
Who was accidentally killed
While doing his duty
NovR. 15th 1914 in his 24th year
Late Farrier South Notts Hussars.

Also Ernest Burton
Father of the Above
Died Dec. 8 1946 aged 80.

At Rest.

Mary-Ann, the wife and mother, did not lie with them, but was cremated so that she could be in real peace at last.

Burton did not believe in God, but his family, at both times equally grief-stricken, said that God had got back at him twice. Once when He took his son, and again when He put out his eye.

Perhaps a thought had been spared for blacksmiths when it said in the Book of Isaiah: 'Behold, all ye that kindle a fire, that compass yourselves about with sparks: walk in the light of your fire, and in the sparks that ye have kindled. This shall ye have of mine hand: ye shall lie down in sorrow.'

Burton never did languish in his waking dreams, but he suffered, all the same.

17

I knew an extremely kind person who believed that everything people said to him was the truth, simply because it pained him to hear it.

Such nobility of spirit could not exist for long. He suffered too much at hearing so many sad stories. I think everyone must have met him, and spilled their troubles. His sensibility was legendary, but for him it was a permanent wound. His receptive and unselective spirit continually bled. He was a real man, being full of sympathy, and because of this people would not leave him alone, but continually kept at him with their plans and complaints.

By liking others and respecting their suffering, he did not hate himself. He considered it infantile to hate oneself, to analyse motives, take oneself to pieces with dislike and hold one's nostrils at the smell. It would mean splitting himself in two, and the part which did the splitting had no real interest in it except self-hatred which, like self-love, is a flame that shrivels you up.

He was tempted, however, to let that other part of himself take him to pieces and tell him the truth. I suspected all the time that he had let it do this to him anyway, and that the experiment had failed. At least he hadn't got what he expected. But he insisted he had kicked that other self out quite early on, and had no more truck with it. I am one person only, he said, not two. I am myself alone and myself only with me, and no other self can be allowed to come on me at this hour. The more you know, especially about yourself, the sooner you grow old.

So he gave himself up to the benefit of other people who, he felt, were less fortunate than he. But if I had been he, which I am not and never would be, he would have laid barbed-wire around his house, bought a gun and shot them down as they came at his defences with wirecutters and implements for tunnelling.

If he had believed in self-preservation he would have filled their ears with his sufferings instead. But he secretly hoped, in his blind pride, to defeat them by endless patience and pity, to go on listening all his life, to bleed them white of the red complaining blood of their speech and change them into ghosts so that he could be free of them at last, and turn himself into a saint.

One morning, just before dawn – he lived alone – he lit the gas to make coffee after spending all night trying to get to sleep – thinking about the numerous years of listening he had done. When the water boiled he turned off the gas and filled the coffee pot. With the usual care he poured a cupful, put in milk, then sugar. He was still listening to the voices, hoping even at this late hour to get something from them.

His friends did not need to be near him any more for him to listen to them speaking their truths. And when they had nothing to say he went on making it up himself, on and on, in their voices, the nonsensical truths they continually talked, and which at last, considering the action he had in mind, were beginning to make sense.

He saw now that the world was full of truth. Everything was the truth. Every word spoken anywhere and everywhere was the truth. He should have been a priest listening to confession in order to find out that the truth was not the truth, that the truth in fact did not exist, no matter how much you worried it, or grieved about it. But it was too late. While the coffee in his cup still steamed, he turned on the taps again and lay down on the floor.

He was a writer, but the more people talked to him, and confessed to him, and complained to him, the less he would write. He felt that every sentence from them took a week off his life, and he was right, for the more he received the stab of their sentences, the more he was driven to take his own life, because he could not think of one sentence to save himself that he had not already heard from somebody else.

18

Burton was working in the blacksmith's shop at the pit one day when a piece of burning steel flew into his eye.

He staggered back and put a hand to the wound. Then he dabbed at it and went on working.

At the end of the shift he walked out as if nothing had happened. He did not go to a doctor, and neither did he claim compensation – which he could have done. He went blind in that eye, and took the piece of steel in it to the grave with him.

He lived many of his days in the thirty years that followed in appalling pain, which almost certainly accounted for much of his harshness and short temper in the latter part of his life, by which time he might otherwise have mellowed a little.

He was no iron man, and felt pain with the same intensity as anybody else. He was also no hero, for if he had been he might have kept a stiff upper lip and been as light-hearted as the rest of his family wanted him to be. Or he would have said nothing unmerciful and allowed them to live as peacefully as they would have liked. But he believed in spreading his suffering, and putting up with it by making others suffer. Whether they liked it or not, they had to share it with him. At the same time they were never allowed to mention the cause of it, in return for which they did not hear it from his own lips either.

He'd sit in a darkened room when he could bear the affliction no longer, a bottle of whisky at his side, and even when he was over seventy I remember being told not to go into the parlour because he wanted to be by himself.

His family said he was not capable of love, that he had never loved anyone and never would, though to me he seemed tender to his wife, and calm enough when I knew him and they were elderly.

Going out together he made Mary-Ann walk some paces behind, and this caused much comment, though he never altered in his habit. At the same time he could not live without her – or let her out of his sight. When she went on a week's visit to her family at St Neots he followed her down after two days, leaving the children (some of whom were grown-up) to fend for themselves.

There was a house at Ramsey where he stayed with Mary Ann's sister, and when he woke up in the top back bedroom he looked out over the foggy dews of the Fens, and saw blue-tits fighting on the tree at the end of the garden. At breakfast, one time when he had a cold, he drank from his own special bottle of 'colic water' which he always travelled with, a sort of horse-medicine he swore would cure everything that a human might be stricken with. He once took his sister-in-law and her husband to dinner at the local hotel, and on seeing so many leftovers lying around he suggested to the manager that he should keep pigs in order to profit by them.

In the prime of their married life Burton gave Mary-Ann as little money as possible to keep all ten. When they lived at Bridge Yard (a house on Wollaton Road between the school and a coal-loading wharf on the canal), she took in washing to try and make ends meet. Her complaints made no difference to Burton, who seemed impenetrable, and couldn't even understand he was being unkind. She needed money for the house, but he had to have cash for beer, without which he could neither work nor live.

Burton was opaque and unjust, but he was a poor man all his life, and though he worked at a skilled trade, he was always on the edge of poverty. He made horseshoes of great beauty and ability and no doubt sold them dirt cheap, even for that time. Only in his late fifties did existence become easier – though not much, for times never stop being hard for the working man. In the thirties there were four other wage-earners in the family, so that the house seemed reasonably well off to me.

But when his children were young they said he took more care at feeding his half-dozen pigs than he did over them. People who came to the house with buckets of slops and baskets of crusts would get a penny or two from Burton, who would tell one of his children to carry them to the sty. On the way there he or she would search for bits still fit to eat, but Burton never knew this, otherwise they would have got a good kick for daring to rob their own father. And nobody would tell him to his face that they were hungry.

He worked unbelievably hard. Blacksmithery was a trade that demanded it, in which it was said that some smiths occasionally went blind from the spirit-breaking labour of their toil. Yet for all that, Burton appeared a sensitive man to me. Perhaps as a child, and a grandchild at that, I was able to get through to a part of him that he could never open to his own children or even to himself. His one good eye, extraordinarily alive, missed nothing. His mouth was permanently ironic, turning down at each end but as if it didn't really want to. Wicked lips, when closed, were ready to play any trick, or to let one be done.

Every face has a fixed look which is not only based on the formation of the features themselves but is also moulded by the qualities of the inner spirit. It was stamped there at some moment of truth, which may have been at the point of conception, when the two expressions on the parents' faces fused into that of the conceived soul. This was modified at the child's shock on coming out of the womb and into the air, and further altered by the environmental pounding of its first few years.

A person can never let go of this self-image by which the inner complex is recognisable to the percipient observer. Burton was too sure of himself ever to think of escaping from his. He simply dug deeper and deeper into it, and stayed that way.

19

In spite of this necessary but unthinking loyalty to his own identity, most of it maintained at the expense of others, Burton's children ended up diffident and civilised, good-natured, and with a sense of humour. This was certainly due more to the benign influence of Mary-Ann than the stern eye and often hard fist of their father.

The youngest of his three sons was also no scholar, and when I was a child and he was about thirty, he asked me to teach him to read. I tried hard to, but it was impossible for a boy of ten to fight against the random core of illiteracy in my parents' families. Eventually, his wife taught him to read and write. He married late, and sang hymns and songs at his own wedding, being the only Burton who had any kind of voice and a fondness for music.

The most consistent charge levelled against Burton was that he 'interfered too much'. Whatever happened in the house and family he would comment on, usually in a derogatory fashion, poking his nose into things with such dominant advice that he was remembered only as a bully by his grown-up children.

There was one of his daughters whom he was not allowed to hit or rail at as a child, for she was a little backward until later in life. Mary-Ann loved her the most, and would not leave her alone for a moment in Burton's presence, but took her everywhere. Nevertheless, she grew up in fear of her father, though with no sign of open resentment like the others. She did not become mentally ill, as she undoubtedly would but for her mother's care, and was able to earn her living and maintain a certain humour against the world. She went occasionally to church, but only after Burton died, for then he no longer paralysed them by his silent presence, or damned them by his nagging. Two of his daughters never married while he was alive – which they blamed on him.

'Burton' is an old gipsy or didacoi name, though I never heard it said that he actually came from such people. Nor did he step out of any entertainment of the Arabian nights, or show much interest in the anatomy of melancholy. I know that when I lived in the Hertfordshire countryside ten years ago the pubs had signs on the doors saying NO GIPSIES OR DIDACOIS SERVED HERE. I suppose the landlord imagined that they posed some threat to himself and his genteel customers.

Didacoi or not, Burton did have a way with animals, horse-shoes, and women. He also smoked, drank, filled himself with fat, and died at nearly eighty. Idleness was hell, and he would rather be ill than idle – though there was never a sickness in his life, because he wouldn't allow it. In his terms of reference there was only a cold or a headache, neither of which was a strong malady, and so were easily cured by waiting for them to go away.

Luckily, they always did. When he woke up groggy and out of sorts the day would break him of it, and by nightfall he would be better from his irreversible dosage of work. Three remedies that kept him fulsomely active were Friar's Balsam, Fuller's Earth, and Epsom Salts. He smoked Robin cigarettes, though often sat at the parlour table making his own. He was a good customer of Shipstones' Ales, and never ate meat and butter at the same meal.

Nobody knows where he has gone to, though some said that there was only one place for a man like him. He's vanished, but not without trace, and since I can't light candles, I write words, for in spite of all that was said about him he was my grandfather on my mother's side.

Not long ago, at the bottom of the dream-pit, I was inside a large barn-like building. Using great force, I twisted a piece of new wood from a banister rail, and it was satisfying to pick at its freshly splintered surface.

I showed it to Burton: 'You see how vigorous and alive the wood is?'

'Yes,' he answered readily, with all-knowing irony, 'but it's rotten. Look at it.'

And staring close I saw that, just beneath its surface, the wood was pullulating with tiny winged insects and maggots.

'Well,' I told him, as usual trying to make the best of something catastrophic, even in a dream, 'David will be able to examine them under his microscope. I've just bought him a new one.'

David is my son. One of his great-grandfathers, and a contemporary of Burton, was a cantor in a synagogue in Bukovina. Burton, happy at the sight of him coming towards us, gave a smile of uncomplicated pleasure that he'd never been able to put on with an adult. The main person in a dream is always oneself, no matter who it is. David was myself as a child in this dream, and also himself as he is now.

One can't have one's grandparents all one's life, for if this were so one wouldn't then have them to look back on, and childhood would not have been what it was. But of all those now dead of my family, Burton is the one whom I would like to know that I had become a writer, and whom I would happily read novels and stories to.

I ought to stop writing about him because I do not want to become in any shade similar, or feel encapsulated by his spirit. He was too real a person, and so I will pull gradually away. With a straightforward tale it would be possible and necessary to become him in order to write about him. I'd feel entirely easy in it, and sense no danger tunnelling my way through such a yarn, because I would be certain to come out empty on the other side.

One's grandparents are more important in every way than one's parents.

20

The truth is difficult to get at, as if it's locked in a near-impregnable first-class Vauban fort that one is only let into on humble sufferance – hauled up the sheer scarps in a wicker basket, as it were. But one doesn't want to go in on such terms or make any fuss about it. Truth comes in flashes, forgotten pictures which it blesses us with. The fact that it comes at all makes it generous.

As an old man of nearly eighty, Burton went to visit one of his married daughters in Kent. It couldn't have been too long before he returned to Nottingham and died, though there was no sign of it until close to the end. He stood with another of his grandsons watching combine-harvesters circling the wheat, and when the field was small some bystanders began throwing missiles at rabbits running for safety.

Burton saw one in the chaff close by and made a grab for it. At that moment a piece of slate smashed into the back of his hand, inadvertently hurled by someone who did not see him.

He made no complaint. He kept his grip on the rabbit, which he hit sharply at the back of the neck and killed. He stood up and said nothing, then walked off with his grandson to the doctor's house a few miles away to get his hand put right, blood trailing on the ground from his shattered veins, the dead rabbit swinging from his pocket.

21

So as not to share the same fate, metaphorically or otherwise, of that erstwhile friend of mine who flipped on the gas-taps, I have to ask sooner or later: 'Where do I begin?'

It comes as something of a shock to realise that I have already done so. The path to truth is well advanced, though little has been said. The mists of uncertainty show how far and wide I have strayed, but broken vision is a promising phenomenon, in that the fabulous can be perceived in it, something that never comes from an open sky or a precise landscape. When all things stand out bright and clear, there is little possibility that one's own personal truth will take shape.

The first stage is over when the taps are tightened in a clockwise direction. One can act when the maps are burned, the plans forgotten, when schemes have disintegrated, and the obscuring particles close in. One does not get an inch closer to truth by the age-old tactic of self-murder. To end life out of despair means that one hasn't even started to sift the galaxies of truth-dust.

One can talk continuously for fifteen hours, and cause whoever listens to commit suicide, but still not touch the central core of boiling fire, nor its periphery, though one's whole life-story might have been through the wringer.

Yet out of this mist a story of sorts may be forming itself, personalities emerging from the amniotic fluid.

22

The fluid is gritty, covers a vast area and goes deep. Sometimes it floods my mouth with a foul taste.

But I won't indulge in autobiography, that flagrant telling of my own flat tale. I refuse to write the Madman's Guide to Europe, or compile a history of the Hundred Years War in ninety-nine pages, though if I scribble about my grandparents and their children I cannot be forced into birth for the crime of going back on my word.

The reliability of these sentences is more uncertain than any map, and they are only to be used with extreme caution. But caution is a bad dream, a high-waisted lady with a withered bust holding in her left hand a flower for Miss Midnight. Is a desire to tell the truth merely a wish to burn oneself prematurely out?

At dusk the grey-white belly and wings of a house-martin flits by the window. The young are being fed in their mud nests under the eaves. Once you leave home, you've got no home: all of them fly south in the autumn, though next year they will return to the exact places in which they spent the summer, except those who die on the way.

Just as each of the numerous families of house-martins is different, to judge by their talk and their coming and going, so can every person say, 'Ours is a unique family because there isn't another one like it.' That may be the only good point about such miniature para-military dictatorships in which the head is imprisoned even more firmly than the rest, though he at least has the dubious pleasure of wielding power. But until the New Age dawns – and its approach has not yet been reported from any distant planet – the importance of families can hardly be overrated.

I know more about the antecedents of Mary-Ann who married Burton, than my other three grandparents, though the information came to me only when both Burton and his wife had been dead twenty years.

A woman from Leeds wrote a letter saying that in a certain novel of mine she had been struck by amazing coincidences that related to her own life. It turned out that the grandfather described in the early chapters resembled a relation of hers called Burton, whom she used to visit with her mother as a child, and also later in her teens.

She described Burton, her mother's uncle by marriage, as a tall, thin, dour man who seemed to have a cast in one eye and was always called by his surname. His family lived in fear of him and, being a child, she also was terrified of such a man.

The last time she saw him was in the late 1920s when he went to Leeds and stayed two nights for the funeral of Mary-Ann's brother, Bill Tokin, who lived at Horseforth and had worked as a railway porter all his life. Bill was a big, rather miserable and overbearing type who was not liked by many. The Tokin men at his funeral were over six feet tall, handsome men with raven-black hair and blue eyes, and Burton stood out among them because, though he was as tall, he had fair hair and brown eyes. She was impressed by the collective height and bulk of these men who filled the small parlour of dead Bill Tokin's house.

On her visits to Engine Town she remembered that Ernest Burton wore a wide leather belt, and was always ready to take

57

it off to members of his family or to his dogs. A funny quirk of his was that he invariably walked many paces ahead of his wife, as though she were not with him at all.

He would, however, put his hand on *her* mother's arm, and still go in front of Mary-Ann. They usually went back to Leeds laden with marrows, potatoes, kidney beans, and rhubarb out of his garden. Burton made a great fuss of her mother, with whom he got on well. He admired her, and treated her as something special, and she was said to be fond of him. He was indeed a peculiar man, though my correspondent added that the Tokins, from whom my grandmother sprang, were said to be a stranger breed still.

23

The memory comes back to me of a seven-year-old boy building roads. I might have been younger, wandering alone to a nearby tip away from any houses, on which only waste sand and factory soot was laid, an area between the narrow River Leen and a few acres of swamp bordering the railway line, closed off from the lane by a stockade of high boards. I could get on to the tip by climbing a tree and leaping over the top of the fence, then scrambling down a huge bank of clean sand and gravel on the other side.

In the light of what I was later to become, such occurrences in childhood seem amusing, though this small laugh is merely to protect me from the daunting stab of whatever was relevant. Yet pulling truth out by the nettleheads so that roots snap free makes me realise that these memories are amusing simply because I imagine other people's smiles if I mention them. My own already exist, and tell me that such laughter only points to another kind of truth.

Sometimes I would use guile instead of brawn, and get into the wasteland by waiting for a lorry to enter the gate. When the driver opened it before going in I would follow suit without being noticed, and hide myself behind rusty, dry-leaved tea-bushes. After he'd left I'd find an old piece of spade and start to build a new road quite independent of the main track of the lorries.

For an afternoon and part of the evening I was in peace, levelling a pile of house-bricks and decorators' rammel, and a mountain of black soot from some workshop chimney, widening and hardening the surface, macadamising my road with spadesful of soot.

Deciding where to guide it was always a problem, though when I came next day to drive it forward another ten or twenty feet, it had been obliterated by lorries that had in the meantime dumped their stuff. I wasn't called upon to commit myself, or to push a road through a morass as I now am, though I was quite prepared to do so had it been either necessary or possible.

In wondering why the lorry-driver had callously buried my road I could only believe that, from the godlike height of his cab, he hadn't even noticed its feeble line. It was too narrow to be of use, or too unreal for him to see. In place of the paved highway I imagined to exist, there was in reality a piece of narrow track that might barely have served as a false lure into rugged mountain country, fit at the most for the feet of men and animals. Yet I wondered why he had tipped his load over it when there was so much unused space round about. Since something in him must have glimpsed the beginnings of a highway, proved by the fact that he had tried to blot it out, I couldn't finally tell whether this disfigurement was to my spiritual gain or not.

In the darkness of childhood I did not go this far in my reasoning, but one step further and I feel certain I would have done. A child is a mystic, and what he lacks in intelligence and worldly knowledge he makes up for in earnestness and depth of feeling.

Every child is a prince ruling over a kingdom of half-dark and half-light, which only the revolution of age can inextricably mix up, and condemn him to the lie that he can recognise day-light when he sees it.

24

When I knew my grandmother she was sixty and had white hair, but in her younger days it had been reddish and golden. Being the youngest of a large family she was a girl of few opinions, but the many virtues she had lasted all her life. She was put into service at thirteen, and a few years later was working as a general help at the White Hart pub in Lenton.

Burton, son of the local blacksmith, got to know her there. He was young and tall, though his strength alone was handsome – his eyes firm, his nose straight, his hair short and fair, a moustache worn as if to balance his strong chin. Like any farrier, he had a permanent spark in his throat from smithing, and no amount of beer could ever put it out. While asking for a pint at the bar he fell in love with this shy, plump girl called Mary-Ann, and told her so.

She was busy and said nothing, and if she believed her ears it didn't seem possible that he was more than joking. But as the weeks went by he said it again and again, not with any sentimental fervour, but straight out, as if he were saying he loved beer or pork.

Being a servant she wasn't able to leave the pub more than once a month, and one day she took a fancy to a pair of black cotton gloves in a newspaper advertisement. Burton was surprised when, after saying he loved her and wanted her to marry him, she pushed a florin over the counter and asked if he'd go and get her a pair of black gloves from a shop down town. They'd cost one and elevenpence, she told him.

She thought he might wait till the weekend to do it, but he downed his pint and went straight away. When he came back two hours later he pushed the gloves across the bar with the florin she'd given him still on top of the packet. The next time he asked her to marry him she said yes.

After her marriage she hardly ever went to church, for fear

of Burton's scorn, though she believed in God, and was certainly superstitious. It is said that lightning never strikes a blacksmith's house, and Burton averred so often enough in a bantering boastful tone when Mary-Ann showed herself full of dread at the onset of a bad storm. She felt that every lightning flash coming from the black sky was especially aimed at her, so maybe it was no bad thing that she married a man who stood in absolute fearlessness of it, though his mockery of the fear she felt did little to comfort her.

But while he was in the house it was true that she wasn't so frightened. When he was at work, however, she would open the front door wide, in spite of the rain driving in, so that if a thunderbolt came spinning with vicious and dreadful power down the chimney and madlarked into the hearth it would be drawn by the gap of light to continue its journey harmlessly into the yard – without exploding and blowing the house to pieces.

Having taken that precaution she would retire to the dark place on the stairs with an oil lamp, even if her grown children were sitting in the kitchen. When the storm's fearful rumbles ceased to penetrate into her hideaway and reach for her soul, she would open the stairfoot door and ask whether it was safe to come out.

She led a blameless life, and no one ever knew what there was for her to be frightened of. If anyone should have been afraid of being struck dead it ought to have been Burton, but Mary-Ann thought that the supernatural power behind the lightning bolts would not bother to sort out the good from the bad on finally deciding to aim a big one at his house. Or perhaps she sensed that if Any Being wanted to get back in the deadliest way at another, it would take the one nearest to him, and she was certainly that person to whom Burton was most attached. The price of marrying anyone is to pay for their sins, but he treated her as he would have treated himself if he had discovered the same weak traits in his own make-up, which is the highest form of injustice.

He derided her soft heart, especially when she couldn't bear to see him kicking the dogs or knocking his children about, so it is possible that she had more humility instilled into her than she had been born with, and therefore more fear of everything. She continually worried, though it was of a sort that would never break her down, and in fact most likely kept her going. It tormented her, yet made her strong, because it demanded such great effort.

She was in many ways weak, but effort is often the only effective fuel of the weak, and a lasting impression is that she must have been as strong as iron to put up all her life with someone as hard as Burton.

When he was about forty she saw him in a pub talking to two women. This was no surprise to her because something had been said already of his carryings on. She walked up to the bar and threatened that if he didn't come home straight away she would go back and set fire to the house.

He laughed, and told her to leave him alone. When she stood there, wondering why she had bothered to tackle him, he pushed her outside with everyone looking on. In her tears she repeated the threat, and though Burton went back to his two women he eventually lost his nerve, afraid that she might actually do as she said.

She was still in the yard when he caught her, not far from the house door. His consciousness roamed around behind his eyes like a tiger unshackled by the chain of words or reason. He grasped her by the hair, dragging her back in a wild rage and spinning her round as his fists flew. The children came up at her screams, and began howling. Burton's last furious punch caught her in the mouth and knocked two of her front teeth out. He then went in and locked the door behind him, staying till conscience nagged sufficiently for him to go and see to her.

Nobody knew why she put up with him. Though so much injustice had been done to her she didn't let anything unjust go by without comment – at least not in my presence. All harshness from without, and uncertainty within, registered on the lines of her brow. Headaches continually plagued her and the daughters. The sons were affected by weak stomachs, which showed how Burton had got on their nerves from birth, though they were all fit men and lived a long time, as it turned out.

Headaches and bad stomachs became a thing of the past when Burton died. His children then took on the residue of toughness and longevity that, perhaps in spite of himself, he left them with.

25

When I built a secret road on the rammel-tip I hoped in my reasonably young heart that a lorry would drive along, and that the man inside would use it to take him to a new place on which he could dump more rubble and add to my highway.

To try and write the truth, and at the same time make it more attractive for those who might read it, would be to commit a lie, an unforgiveable act when set on a self-conscious furrowing. To refuse the responsibility of a lie means pushing art out of the way, for it is only possible to create art when seeking to make raw truth believable.

I wanted to make a road for the other people to use. But the zone of ground between river and railway, long since covered in factory warehouses, figures once more in my landscape of truth.

My mother knew one of the lorry-drivers, and even before I used to go there alone I went to it holding her hand, younger than seven years of age. She waited for him outside, and when he came he would open the gate for us. They were both young, and he must have been good enough looking, for he preferred to talk rather than eat, and I watched him open his lunch-box and take out an apple and a piece of cake.

Any attempt to soften what I am about to say will put me at the beginning of a lie. Nevertheless, I will lift belief to a higher plane by making it dependent on truth and not lies. It is as if truth were a crime that I am burning to commit, but the only crime would be to distort the truth knowingly no matter what amount of lip-service is paid to lies. But I am intending to

63

commit this crime for myself alone, and not for the benefit of anyone around me. It might feel like a sudden advent of religion, when God is seen to be of Truth, his stern and precipitate appearance promising me an increase of faith in myself providing I placate him with my own hollow spirit by the time I have finished writing.

I wasn't even hungry, but did as I was told and went to the other end of the tip with my apple and cake. After I had eaten I started to build my first road, and was lost in the work of it when my mother said we must go because the gate was about to be locked. I took her hand, but she was too distracted to be with me on the way back, because she must have been worrying about my father. She needn't have bothered though, because she had, after all, only taken me out for a walk.

26

When Howard was nine and out to buy a comic he saw a trolley-bus on Wollaton Road whose poles had come loose. Running across to look he was struck by another bus, which so mangled his leg that he had to have it off.

His father was Oswald, Burton's second son who had married a Catholic girl called Nellie. While the whole family mourned the loss of Howard's leg, they tried to console the parents by saying that at least he hadn't been killed – while Burton was heard to remark that it might have been better if the poor little bogger had. The only reply to shut him up was when Ivy said that though *he* had but one eye he still liked living. He didn't deny this, but went on thinking he was right.

Howard sat in the parlour because he could not tolerate the light, much like Burton for another reason. He passed the time sifting piles of silver paper collected by all the family so that he could take it to the hospital on days when he went for treatment. He had been learning the piano but wouldn't play it any more, sat on its stool unable to lift the lid.

He could no longer go to St Mary's Roman Catholic School on Derby Road. Sometimes he sat on a chair in the garden, watching the traffic go by, an active boy who had been shattered into stillness by a blow he could not understand.

Ivy took him to the Elite Cinema a year after the accident. In the middle of the film he complained of pain in his leg. He was a stoical boy, so she knew something was wrong, and took him home. In bed he sang beautiful songs, words and music of his own making, his face animated but his eyes closed. It was impossible not to weep on hearing them. He died a fortnight later with a heart no longer strong enough to support him.

Howard was a year older than me and I had not been encouraged to play with him because I was considered too rough. I called at the house some time after he had died, on my way to Engine Town. It was early morning, and Nellie was still in bed, while Oswald was getting ready to go on duty as a sort of guardian on the nearby canal, where he worked because there was no longer much for him to do as a blacksmith.

He was a tall, thin man like Burton, but there was a more human and vulnerable handsomeness about him, a sensitive enough man because he had some of the Tokin complexity and pity in him passed on by his mother. He told me to finish the bacon left from his breakfast, and I looked at the plate of rinds with the hard cold fat still attached, and the slice of bread he generously cut. Although I hadn't eaten I couldn't touch it. The food was good, and in another house I would have scoffed it, but my appetite would not rise.

Nellie tried to console herself by going down town to St Barnabas' Cathedral, and by drinking bottles of stout, but the grief was so great that nothing succeeded. When we met on the street she stopped and took my hand, holding it in her warm one. She was a gentle person, with long dark ringlet-hair, her face bright and eager with a despair she would not let go of. Her melodious voice was almost breaking as she asked: 'Where do you think Howard is now?'

I was embarrassed, and didn't want to remind her of his death, because she knew very well where he was. I stood still and said nothing.

She eventually let go: 'He's in Heaven, that's where he is!'

There was nothing Nellie wanted more than to follow him. When death takes someone for no reason, in a situation other than war or battle, it often kills the will to resist a similar fate in those close by. Yet Nellie was allowed to live on into old age, and had no other child.

I wondered why Howard ran into the road to be maimed and killed, what he was running towards or escaping from. Maybe Jesus did take him to his bosom, as Nellie liked to think, meaning as far as I was concerned that it was pure senseless chance. Burton felt the echo of his own dead son, stood up even straighter when the shock began to gnaw and it was seen in his face as one more blow against the family.

Nellie made me feel helpless, so I stopped being sorry and avoided her in that ruthless way children have when they are afraid. It wasn't my fault Howard had died, and I couldn't bear to have his mother wonder why I was alive and he was dead. I'm sure she never thought this, for her soul was good, but I felt it myself. In any case, she did not believe he was finally dead. He was in Heaven, and had been taken away for a while – forty-five years to be exact.

The Burtons felt that, because she was a Catholic, she brought colour into their lives and gave them something to talk about. There was always a need to get off the eternal subject of their father; and godless people such as Burton are tolerant enough of those who have a religion to look up to, as long as it is not the one *they* were born with and feel guilty at not showing respect for. It is one step up the ladder from sloth to myth.

There was no doubt that Oswald loved Nellie all his life and pitied her more than he did himself for the tragedy she'd been forced to share. She was ill and partially paralysed for her last dozen years, and Oswald was a strong man who generously wore himself out nursing, lifting, doing everything for her. Over seventy years old, he fell dead from a heart attack one morning. He had meticulously prepared his garden for the spring planting of vegetables, and all the seeds for it were laid out by the back step of his prefab at Bilborough. Nellie lived two more years, and left a thousand pounds to the church.

It seems centuries since I saw them, almost as if what occurred never happened, events slung up from the great unconscious into a spreading and ramifying dream that for once I can remember. Burton lost another grandson called Phillip, the youngest child of Edith, who at the age of five fell into a canal and was drowned. He slipped in quietly one winter's morning, and his friends of the same age ran away frightened, not telling about it till they were questioned in the evening.

It is bound to be little else but death and turmoil in a backward scoop to the jungle of where one came from. Death is rolling towards everyone underfoot. I am deceived at the solid feel of the earth – which is waiting to pull me like a trapped fox into its soil. Death is the final black clapper of life, and maybe it doesn't bother me because I can't bear to think about it. It might also be that those who see death as the end are the ones who fear it most.

As for calling that dreamlike far-back zone – in which the first-seen people of my life appeared – a jungle, it certainly was exactly the opposite of a desert, due to its green richness and many traps, and its instilling of lifelong love. Those whom I knew so well are part of my corporate identity. Such mixing creates the mystery that makes every soul unique, and safe beyond the deathly probing of sociological scholarship. They are the segments that fix the truth of anyone, and it can be done in no other way.

When that line of thick forest is stabilised at my back, the way will be clear before me. Seed from its trees will drift off and fertilise the plain in front, so that my heart will burst when I cross it. One does not exist unless the heart is full. One crumbles into dust, and that is the only real death.

27

I suppose I was born into the world wanting to love my parents. I knew my father wouldn't like my mother to be seen talking with somebody else, and realised how silent I had to keep about her conversations with the lorry-driver by the rammel-tips. It was difficult to look my father in the eye, and when he hit her for what I knew to be true I had reason to hate him for the rest of his life, though a few days later I had forgotten all about it.

It taught me to keep a secret and initiated me into the feat of being able to prevent ice from melting in the middle of a fire. I developed cunning and deceit, though it might have come later, or started much earlier. Still, I couldn't hold it against her for doing it on my father, if that is what happened, for whoever lived with him had to survive, and that was a fact.

When a little truth has been found there is no reason to condemn people. They existed and did what they did only so that one day I would be able to find the truth. How else can you look at it if you are continually fighting against falsehoods in yourself?

The liars who run society can condemn people. Let the judges and magistrates go rotten with injustice and iniquity. Those who seek after truth have no right to condemn, while those who think they have found it do little else. Perhaps those who search for the truth lack the courage or are too lazy to condemn. One small truth leads to another, and once it begins there is no stopping. It is difficult to say whether seeking after truth is a self-abuse of the spirit, or a holy flight of fancy that grows into a way of life – which is something to be prevented at all costs.

But nothing is too painful if it can be remembered. Memories have already been screened and released in the pit of the mind before they are splashed on to the brain with such force that they cry out to you, and make you cry out when you feel them. They are sent as the only signposts to truth, and to remind you that truth is still possible. If you ignore them they go away either gracefully or with flesh in their mouths, but they always return in another form, at another time, behind another picture, possibly more acceptable, yet maybe with even sharper teeth.

Memories are part of yourself and, peaceful or not, your eternal friends, for if they lead you to some sort of truth it is only with the object of completing your wholeness, the humanity that will protect you against the world while at the same time making you more vulnerable to yourself.

I used to believe that as far as getting at the truth was concerned my subconscious could be relied on, but now I know that such a way is not for me. Waiting year after year for the subconscious to spew out its truth is a negative attitude that has to be overcome by a deliberate and forceful attempt to get at the truth in other ways, for the subconscious can be just as big a liar as the most wordy politician.

At the same time the subconscious should be held in awe and respect. It has power, its own rights, an entire republic. Through it a man is capable of doing evil if he recognises what his subconsious is prompting him to do yet tells those around him that he intends to act otherwise – and even persuades himself of it. Under the machinations of self-control he hides the progress of what destiny intends for him.

In other words he is able to let his subconscious do its subterranean work at the rate it will be most effective and deadly, in the way primal human matter works out its own evolutionary role. Having mastered patience and wisdom, he may decide to let it go into evil instead of good, becoming sly and full of such self-control that it is nothing more than perversity and malice.

Once the subconscious gets you in its power it is impossible to escape, or to disown it if it threatens you with harm, or to save those whom you ought to love. An intelligent man can thus be taken over by a wolf. He perceives everything but is controlled by the mechanism of an animal, and has no defence against it.

Driving back alone in the dark from London I lost all idea

of where I was going and where I was coming from. It was not a new feeling. I've had it often before, of not belonging anywhere, or to anyone except myself. It is a precious and salutary sensation, like driving an aeroplane towards the Himalayas. The soft roar of the Peugeot lulled me on the motorway. I passed the tail-lights of another car as if they were sparks.

It was like lifting into the sky. In a motor-car one flies along, encapsulated in a comfortable seat, breathing stale air, all heaters burning, maps locked in the glove-box, headlights shining on a road that does not alter and so gets you nowhere. I am in a womb, sheltered, warm, and only half safe, waiting for the death-crash of being born, or the birth-crash of being dead, hoping whatever happens that I have loved my parents.

28

A man called Bill Goss drove up from Cambridgeshire in a Rolls-Royce to visit the Burtons at Engine Town. Goss's wife was a niece of my grandmother, and his family enjoyed their trips to Nottingham in the thirties.

He parked his car on the unpaved lane, by a fence that stood at a crazy angle but never fell down. I felt sick when he took me for a ride so we had to turn back before getting very far. It wasn't that my squeamish soul disliked his smooth machine, because I'd go pale in trolley-buses as well. It was simply that my inherited Tokins's stomach played up to its role.

As a young man Bill Goss opened a small shop in a village near Peterborough. A craftsman saddler (eight stitches to the inch), he later stocked push-bikes and did repairs. He then took up cars via motor cycles, and went on to install the first petrol pump in his village. After a while he moved into larger premises, and began to deal in second-hand vehicles.

Perhaps the Rolls-Royce was one of these, but its presence in the lane by Burton's house made them seem fabulously rich, though Goss and Burton were equal enough when they strolled down the lane together. But people who sold bicycles and cars looked to me like the gaffers of the world. They had no worries because they could buy a packet of fags without thinking twice about it, and didn't need to know where their next meal was coming from since it was waiting for them on a warmed-up plate.

You could see it in their faces as they climbed from the car with royal nonchalance when they arrived before Sunday dinnertime, wearing caps and trenchcoats, scarves and shawls. Nobody held it against them, and there was a friendly atmosphere at Engine Town for this exotic branch of the family, good sports and fine mixers who made a more than fair living in the motor trade.

Charles and Mary Tokin shipped over from County Mayo during the potato famine of the 1840s and settled in St Neots with their six sons. For luggage they had a trunk, a hat-box, and a score of bundles.

The family had owned land in Ireland, but were dispossessed by the English. The women were red-haired and goodhearted, while the men were all tall, raven-haired, hard-working, and proud in their loss.

Three of the sons went on the land as agricultural workers, while the father and the rest became railway labourers in the days when tracks were being laid all over England and tens of thousands of navvies were needed for the rapid shifting of earth, clay, and stone. It was as if the government of the day did nothing to curb the excesses of the Irish famine simply to drive enough men of muscle and intelligence to England at a time when the native energies of the Industrial Revolution were on the wane.

A grandson of Charles Tokin met and married Anne Gilbert of St Neots, and one of their children, born about 1870, was Mary-Ann whose fate led her to Nottingham and into the arms of Ernest Burton.

The Tokins were always a family for railways, and maybe it is their blood that stirs in me when I hear train hooters in the night, noises which bring unquiet longings and fix me so much into the network of the world that I am never happily settled in the place where I happen to be.

Of Mary-Ann's two brothers who worked on the railway, Bill was a porter in Leeds, and Ted had a similar job seventy miles down the line at Grantham. The same green hat-box that had come over from County Mayo was filled with Fresh Yorkshire bread baked by Grandma Tokin at Leeds in the morning, and sent in the guard's van to Grantham.

Ted had a boy cycle home with the hat-box, whereupon his wife returned it to the station laden with new-culled Lincolnshire vegetables. These were put into the luggage van of the next train making the right connections with Leeds, and sent back up in the afternoon. This specimen of inter-family co-operation went on for over twenty years, and Bill, at the Leeds end, was the man whose funeral Burton was seen at with Mary-Ann in the twenties.

There are many such tales bursting from the genealogical rigmarole of the Tokins's line, telling of the 'queer streaks' certain limbs of it had. Maybe Burton felt out of it among that numerous lot.

Another grandson of the first itinerant Tokin from Ireland became a prosperous builder. At sixty-eight he threw up normal domestic life, left his wife and three daughters, and went into the nearest workhouse much as another sort of man might enter a monastery.

A photograph taken during his sojourn there shows a large, broad-faced, flat-nosed man, a Tolstoyan figure with a bushy white beard, wearing a workman's cap. Hands clasped, half-sitting on a full dustbin, he stares at the camera with an air of philosophical contentment. Behind is a flight of steps and propped against a wall near by is a long-poled sweeping brush I'm sure he never used. The sun shines as if on no one else in that place, and the photo is a good quality memento mounted on a piece of board. Between the name of the Leeds firm and a royal crest it says: PHOTOGRAPHERS TO THE LATE QUEEN.

He had ordered the cameraman in for himself alone, and

72

paid out of his own pocket, for he was rich by any standards. When he died at the age of eighty he left £60,000 to the workhouse, and not a penny to his wife and daughters.

29

Ever since I can remember I have wanted to leave home, to pack up and go. This desire to tread places other than the one I lived in was so deeply implanted that it gave more power to the womb than was good for me, making it hard to avoid reckoning with. The only real journey away from it is death, which merely takes one back to it.

I also wanted to tell people things that they would believe in, a fatal (though honest) admission from someone who is searching for the truth. The wish to convince them makes it impossible for me to get at the truth. One can only state the truth as it appears to oneself, and if others get comfort out of recognising it, then my difficulties are honoured. But I cannot claim that my own truth is good for anyone else – otherwise I run the risk of them turning on the gas taps like the friend of mine already mentioned.

A desire to tell the wrong kind of truth manifested itself at an early age, when I was fascinated by the news being read on the wireless. What was said seemed of high interest and importance, dealing as it did with frightening items of oncoming war. I thought that the man allotted to make such announcements must be a great person indeed. But it was a phase of listening to his master's voice which I soon threw off, though when my mother in an odd moment asked what I wanted to do when I grew up I confessed I'd like to be a news reader.

At eight years of age I used to go to a 'dinner centre' during the midday break from school to have a free hot meal. I went in at the first sitting, and then came out with the rest so that the second hungry group could take our places. For some reason I was possessed to put my head to the window and, though it was shut, shout through the glass, so that I could be heard clearly, all the rich swearwords I had so far learned.

The clatter within went silent at my bizarre and extensive vocabulary, and I took it to mean they were actually listening to what I had to say, so continued bawling obscene nonsense to my first captive audience. When one of the serving women could stand it no longer she came and punched me away from the window until I went off, bewildered and only slightly ashamed.

That was my first taste of wanting to become a writer, and an incipient edging towards the desire for truth. Though it was the false kind, yet it is the first sort one encounters on the long road towards real truth. In any case I had with unknowing perception equated as early as could possibly be expected the news coming over the radio with common irrelevant obscenities.

If and when one attains truth it can never be spectacular or in any way comforting. Everyone is born dead, and the quest for truth is no more than a search to restore life to body and soul. As soon as a person feels the desire for truth beginning to stir within him, in no matter what subconscious or underhand way, he is starting to become alive. One is only alive when the search for truth begins.

To question every single point of existence demands a fundamental stability of the heart. One must know not only why one is alive and inhabiting the earth but also why one will perform the next simple action coming into one's mind. It is an attempt to perceive clearly the connection between the two, and to find a common formula uniting them. Until one can do this one is only half alive, but until one begins to embark on this search one is not alive at all.

We are born alive as infants but quickly become dead – after the first smack and cry for air – even though the flesh still moves. But if one was born alive and then becomes dead, one does not live again until the search for truth begins. The only truth from a dead man who has not set out on a search for the truth is that which he shouts in an incantatory fashion when dancing on the grave of his alive self that he killed because he despises the truth. This state also is part of me. This rhythmic inspirational speech is the kind of truth that can never be relied upon to protect the creative spirit. One is afraid because it is God's truth but not Man's, and what use is God's truth to a man? It moves the poet and the shaman but will not affect the person who feels the acid of self-knowledge eating through his stomach.

It is often necessary and satisfying to spew forth the golden words that shift other people, but one needs an opening to the words that move oneself. Is this wanting too much? Is it a betrayal of one's own spirit to hope for this further truth which seems to be a desire to unite the two?

There are more questions than answers in any quest for the truth. If not, mistrust that truth. But a beginning has been made. To hope for progress is to deny the absolute value of what one is striving for. Such a journey breaks the heart, but a broken heart means that chains are snapping. It is a painful liberation of the spirit. If a person suffers through love or from treachery so that the heart is broken (as it is called) people pity him. They should celebrate and envy him, for his spirit is one move nearer to freedom.

Whatever is done to the heart, and whatever the heart does back, it must be trusted and obeyed absolutely. The only protector is your own heart. It will lead you into the wilderness, but carry you through peril and despair. And if it finally betrays you, you will only have lived in the way you were meant to live.

One sometimes starves in order to prevent the spirit withering away, but one continually searches for food.

30

Mary-Ann never turned a beggar away from the door, and solemnly told me never to do so, either.

If there wasn't a penny to give she'd make a cup of tea, or fetch some bread and fat bacon from the pantry. I didn't know how uncommon a trait it was, though it certainly rubbed itself off on her daughters, because when a man walked along our backyard in the hard-up thirties calling out if anybody could spare a cup of tea for a bloke on the tramp my mother would shout from the back door, or through the window if it was summer: 'Come on, then, duck, and let's see what we've got' – though only if my father wasn't there, which went to show in my eyes how good the women were but not the men.

Being a child of parents with widely differing souls, I sometimes follow the precepts of one, and occasionally the uncharitable response of the other, never knowing what I am going to do till I do it. Burton would certainly have bawled a beggar away from his door, telling him to go and find work if he wanted anything to eat.

Any civilising influence in my life could only have come from Mary-Ann Tokin. It was she alone who suggested I do my best to get into a grammar school instead of slogging off to work at fourteen. I think that since her grandson Howard had already died – and the same track had been broached for him – I was the next one suitable.

So on a wet autumn morning I sat in a room of Nottingham High School to do the tests. The atmosphere seemed quite outside me, though I was there with a couple of friends and didn't feel particularly uneasy. The problems were like pages of Chinese ideographs, and I could make nothing of them at first because I had gone through no preparation beforehand. I can't say that I expected to pass, though after puzzling out some of the answers I hoped that by a miracle I would do so.

The rain was stultifying during the hour it took. My feet

were saturated because I wore plimsols, though I soon ignored the discomfort and got stuck in. Nothing could have put me into that school, for even if I'd had a vague chance of getting through this troubling initiation, my spirit wasn't ripe for it. I didn't want it, and it didn't want me, and I believe we were made to sense this by the fools walking about in caps and gowns – which seemed a senseless piece of ritual and intimidation to me and my friends, like something thrown up from the magistrates' court or the Spanish Inquisition. Certainly we had not seen the like of it before. So there was no hard feeling on my side, because when told that I wouldn't be going to such a school I had no regrets.

But I took the test again a year later, and failed that too, proving to me for the last time that I wasn't the right material for higher education. My grandmother may have been disappointed, though I never saw any sign of it.

The experience certainly put me against any form of examination for children. Yet at that time I would have gone on taking any number had there been a chance of getting into a school where French was taught. I felt I was made for something better than what I was heading for, but there did not appear to be any obvious or seemingly possible method by which I could advance in the proper direction and break through.

31

The only time Mary-Ann slipped off her track of high principles was when she spent the remaining week's budget-money on one-armed bandits at some beer-off in Radford, where she had called on her way home with the Co-op groceries. One of her daughters talked her into coming out, saying that otherwise Burton might get to know. But she didn't leave until every last penny had gone.

When someone told him, he took it as an act over which he had no control, and therefore one temptation against which Mary-Ann could not have been expected to show much sense either. In other words, he thought it a bit of a joke, saying: 'Well, I'll be boggered!' – though keeping a tighter grip on her from then on in case she got into debt from it and had them run out of house and home by the bum-bailiffs.

Mary-Ann knew who'd shopped her, because while she was busy at the handle she'd seen Florrie Voce's face reflected in the glass. When tackled about it later Florrie denied it all, but called Mary-Ann an old cow for accusing her of such a thing. Normally good-natured and pacific, Mary-Ann went into the house, and came out with a cup, which she threw with full force and deadly aim at Florrie who was hanging washing up in the yard.

The group of houses abutted the school, and the silence of the classrooms was shattered by a squealing such as could only come from a pig in the process of being slaughtered, or a person whose throat was being unjustly cut. A young lady teacher, rattled by the sound, sent one of Mary-Ann's daughters out to see what was the matter.

Such noise from Bridge Yard was not unusual, but this time it was prolonged for what seemed beyond reason – it being that the cup hurled by Mary-Ann had caught Florrie full in the eye, and cut her both above and below it. A policeman was fetched, and Mary-Ann had to appear at the Guildhall on a charge of breaching the peace and common assault, for which she was fined the sum of £2.

Not that this caused any final rupture between the two women, because a few years later Florrie Voce came to Oliver's funeral and was the loudest wailer at it. They knew that you couldn't make enemies in your own backyard, though you had your ructions now and again. And a £2 fine would never convince Mary-Ann that she'd paid for the cardinal sin of committing violence on a neighbour, a pass she'd got herself into which was right out of character, and which she never did again.

She was a kind, hardworking woman, and thought more about other people than herself. Because of this she was seen as

78

a simple person – a deceptively simple judgement which isn't worth much comment.

She used to collect the coloured cards from Burton's cigarettes and store them in the spice cupboard. They lay there for weeks and months until she had enough to make it worth while presenting them to me in an empty Robin packet. They were impregnated with the smell of curry and pepper, aloes and cloves, sage and thyme. A few years before she died she gave the same cupboard to me and I kept my first collection of books in it.

With a touching and solemn expression she also gave me a stick of oak about six inches long, no more than a piece of kindling, assuring me that it had been part of the ship in which the Good Lord Nelson died. She had paid the exorbitant sum of sixpence for it to some cunning old robber who had once come to her door. I don't remember what happened to it. No doubt I treasured it for a while, then lost it on the long road my itching feet have since travelled.

It is good for the self-confidence of a child to be spoiled when young. The awful word 'spoil' only means love and care, and freedom from unreasonable restrictions so that any good qualities can develop. To do good is the only way to teach others to do good, and to spoil is not to ruin, for it gives a child a sense of his own significance that will strengthen him to face the world and survive.

The reason people don't know what they want, and therefore do not know what to do at certain vital moments of their lives, is because they were told too often as children exactly what they could have and do, and not left enough to their own usually innocent choices. One sees it all the time, even on the streets.

Parents may spoil a child yet not ruin it, though many are too frightened or ignorant to try what is new or relaxed. It is usually left to the grandparents, who need to love a child in order to go on living themselves, and who often spoil grandchildren to make up for having been too harsh with their own. They can also spoil a grandchild so as to make life hard for its parents when that child grows up and begins to assert itself, but that is another matter, and nothing to do with the relatively uncomplicated Burton morality.

Grandmother Burton used to make her own rugs, sat by the fire on winter evenings with a large piece of sacking pulled over her knees. Near her chair were two or three baskets of rug clippings, cut into pieces by herself and her daughters from rags and cast-offs. They were sorted into a few basic colours, from which she planned out the rough patterns.

The result was crude and of a primitive spectrum, but there was always something warm underfoot to stand on in the kitchen – though as rugs they were never considered fine enough for the parlour, in which was laid a large piece of coconut matting. These rugs were her only art form, if they can be called such, and I suppose the designs she concocted from these mounds of vari-coloured clippings gave as fair a picture of her inner mind as one was ever likely to get.

On a summer's afternoon (when her rugs would hang on an outside line to air) I can smell newly-baked bread coming from the heated oven. In a state of grace I get that warm and floury whiff as my grandmother laid the tins on the table. I shall always be able to smell it, as if no one else can, and as if I am the last person in the world to recall it.

Mary-Ann, in saying goodbye, used a refrain that came over from Ireland with her mother: 'God between ye and all harm,' she said – and meant it.

32

Burton was always looking for something bigger than he was to break himself against, though he would have perished rather than admit to such a thing.

He never did find that bigger force. He looked for it, and at the same time kept it at bay with fundamental Burton guile. The closest he got was when he met and married Mary-Ann

Tokin, and she would never admit to it either, though she may have thought about it from time to time.

When Burton died, he died in bed, and all his guts came up, red and black, through his mouth. Like any blacksmith, he kept his silence, knowing that Old Nick had got him at last. And Old Nick was riding a horse that had been shod by somebody else, a fact which accounted for the look of shock on Burton's face.

Just after he died Mary-Ann said to one of her daughters that she wanted to go herself, that there was nothing to live for now that he had gone and she had lasted long enough to see him at rest in his grave.

She died in her sleep a year later. There was no place on earth for her without him, just as there had been no peace on earth for her with him. What greater love is there than that?

All I can do to end this portion and theirs is to paraphrase some lines taken from a one-time gravestone in West Bridgeford church, chiselled in 1785:

'They fell like Autumn Fruit, that mellowed long,
  Much wondered at because they dropped no sooner.
  Fate wound them up for three score years and ten;
  Yet freshly ran they on some winters more,
  Till like a clock, worn out with beating time,
  The wheels of weary life at length stood still.'

33

A circle is a straight line to me. A straight line is a circle. My desire forms a straight line, my thoughts run in a circle. The circle imprisons me, the straight line takes me out of it. But I always return to the circle, if only to embark once more on a straight line. The circle is my bloodstream, pumped through the heart. The straight line is the invisible path I follow. The sun is a circle; a tree is a straight line. The world is a circle at the equator; the horizon is straight when I look at it from a hilltop. My sphincter is a circle; my penis is straight. A circle is not a straight line to me; a straight line is not a circle. The straight line of my desire breaks out of the circle. In searching for truth, whether it takes me on a straight line, or endlessly round in a circle, I am no longer a prisoner. My emblem is that of a straight line through a circle. Will the straight line ever leave the circle behind? The circle is my fundamental self. The straight line is my searching spirit. The circle pushes the straight line forward. The straight line drags the circle with it. They are eternally locked together.

PART TWO

34

My father's parents died soon after I was born, so what their first names were I don't know – and I saw no photographs of them. His family stories were unreliable or totally false, though it is certain that *his* father was an upholsterer from Wolverhampton in Staffordshire who, when he came to Nottingham, fitted out a workshop and 'showroom' on Trafalgar Street in Radford.

He was small in stature and had a short, pointed grey beard, and was said to be a hard and excellent worker except when he took to the whisky, though he rarely did so to the extent of getting blind drunk. Like all the Sillitoes he was tight-lipped, certainly not of the tribe that drinks beer or breathes with their mouths open.

He married a Nottingham girl called Christine Blackwell, whose first name only slips into mind as I write. By all accounts he did not treat her well. She came from a family of cigarette and cigar manufacturers and retailers, and had six sons and two daughters – eight being the figure of plenty in those days.

After he died his offspring were pleasantly surprised to learn that he had been the owner of several slum houses in Wolverhampton, and when these were sold by common filial agreement each flush heir received the sum of £40. To anguished cries that they had been robbed by thieving solicitors (and it really seemed that they had) they spent it in a few weeks to drown their grievance. My father, however, put his portion in an envelope and folded it for safety into his waistcoat pocket, snug notes read to be used for a rainy day.

Employed as an exterior decorator, he was set to work high up a factory wall. It was dry weather, and a smell of suds and swarf came out of the window where he was painting on his piece of plank, himself and colour pots inadequately suspended by pulleys and a rather unstable set of ropes.

Shifting cautiously to one end of it, the contraption began to sink. His view of traffic passing below was a comfort to his precariousness, but that sickening look at it when he should have tried to grasp one of the ropes was a big mistake.

He spun thirty feet, landing stunned and crippled on the ground, covered in a spectrum of paint. By the time he reached hospital his clothes had dried hard as boards. They were cut open and prised off, and when he came back to consciousness the envelope with the money still in it was by his bedside. A few weeks later he hobbled out to spend it, before worse could happen.

One of his brothers was a lace-designer, two were uphol-sterers, and two became managers of butchers' shops. They had nothing to do with the Burtons, imagining themselves a few steps above that sort of uncouth beer-drinking person. Yet neither did the Burtons get much value into their clan when my father married a daughter from it, because he was a man with neither craft nor calling, a labourer who was often unable to find any work at all.

He had been stricken with that disease of malnutrition and neglect known as rickets. It was a mystery why this should have been so in a family which was never badly off, though explanatory whispers put it down to the fact that my father was the youngest child. His brothers and sisters being grown up, he was unwanted and uncared for. The fable goes that he was stuck in a high chair as a baby and more or less forgotten for several years. When he was taken down he could not walk, and had to get about with irons on his legs until he was thir-teen.

At that age he was sent to school, with the help of two sticks, but a few months later his father ended this noble at-tempt to begin his education, so that he could stay at home and help in the shop. The hard work of shifting and carrying upholstered furniture made him immensely strong in the arms and shoulders, and by this he was qualified to labour satisfactorily until the end of his life.

He never talked of his parents. He felt deeply that one should 'honour thy father and thy mother', but knew with truth that he could not do so. The fact bred bitterness in him, for he certainly needed the luxury of such sentiments.

But he did not complain and that, under the circumstances, was quality enough. He contented himself with cursing the Burtons at every opportunity, both to get back at my mother, as if in some way blaming her for his own birth, and also trying to make them pay for his parents' deficiencies. He was so full of shame at such a thing having been done to him that he couldn't even talk about it.

Maybe he sensed that one should not destroy one's parents, no matter what they had done. You destroy them only to become them, and I don't think he wanted to do that. But his lack of intelligence was directly linked to the amount of care he had not received as a baby and a child. Screaming his guts out for food, he had been ignored by his demented or indifferent mother until he was too exhausted to care.

None of his first questions were answered, nor those that came later, so he did not grow up with that minor civilised grace of curiosity. He was able to seek intelligent directions regarding the work he had to do, otherwise it was a case of 'see all, hear all, say nowt' – with no compensation of self-expression.

He did not have the ability to tell much that was interesting, and merely enjoyed the syntactical equipment to swear or give orders to children. If the intelligence he had been born with had by any chance survived this early neglect it might have made him more disturbed than he actually turned out to be. And the kindness and generosity that did survive only served to torment him after he had bullied someone unjustly.

The one spiritual development possible was into ill-temper, melancholia, and obstinate self-spiting stupidity – all of which qualities, built into his congenial nature, he could in any case have done without. He was fastened in his high chair and unable to escape, an infant of sensibility (as all infants are) who did not even have the freedom of the jungle. People invariably suffer more from the torments inflicted by those who are too civilised to know how despicably savage they are.

His mother, having lived to be an old woman, went to sleep one night and woke in the morning with one of her eyes gone. So spin the family tales. The other was all right, but the lost luminary orb had fallen back into its socket and was never found again. She died a few months later, and it was said that her husband, as old as he was, had killed her by kicking her down the stairs, thus denying her the opportunity of dying from the cancer with which she was suffering.

35

My father gave little sign of being connected to his past. He did not need to, since it was in all the lines of his face and in every strand of his black hair. He mentioned that some grandfather (or maybe great-grandfather, he seemed by no means certain) had been the first man to paint on silk – perhaps some trades union banner. I was assured that such a feat had been impossible up to that time. Another member of the family was said to have played the violin in a theatre orchestra of Wolverhampton or Birmingham.

I thought these stories were false, but never asked an uncle to settle my mind because I didn't want to put such questions that would make me seem ridiculous in their staid eyes. Apart from the fact that they might laugh at such preposterous ideas coming from my father, I did not care to test his standards of truth, and didn't think his stories were all that important anyway.

Still, they showed that my father was the sort of person who clung to such legends as a means of preserving a few rags of family identity. At the same time he was a grown-up who, having all power and some knowledge, didn't need to do any such thing. Mostly I thought he was lying in order to entertain us children, but it might be that events simply take on more colour to an illiterate because that is his way of remembering them. Unfortunately I tended to disbelieve most of what was said. Historical circumstances enabled me as a child to feel superior to him, due to the fact that I had been instructed in how to read and write.

When one of his more educated brothers told me the following story there was no question of not believing him. A young man of the family called Lewis went to Oxford when he was eighteen. He was said to have been a brilliant student, though somewhat black in his melancholy, as he was indeed swart in complexion. There were positive high hopes of him, but he died of a brain tumour at twenty.

As the mother's favourite son he was to have made all her earthly and matrimonial sufferings worth while. In the bleak twilight of life still left, though she wasn't much older than forty, she thought to console herself with an enlarged oleograph of him and the contents of his box which had been sent back from university after the funeral.

She craved a look at his possessions, expecting a feast of recollection for her sombre mind. The husband was willing to leave her locked in grief, imagining such rich territory to be fair exchange for the freedom to live more openly with his mistress. But all the box contained was a leather bag of sovereigns and a collection of pornographic books, as well as the manuscript of a short and obscene novel called *When the Diligence Stopped for Dinner* written during a six week holiday in Switzerland. This work was burned, along with the rest of the offensive matter, and his mother contrived to believe for the rest of her life that he had walked the ways of the Lord and died pure-hearted.

It was on the same journey that Lewis happened to visit the bear garden at Berne. Old Bruin had its place on the city's coat of arms, and several live specimens were sumptuously accommodated by the authorities in the Bärengraben just across the river.

Someone bet an English officer that he didn't have the courage to get inside the den and climb from one cage to the next. He accepted the wager, and on his progress fell into the pit, and could not get out before a huge male Bruin lumbered over to attack him.

The officer put up a tremendous fight for his life, but was eventually torn to pieces – while Lewis and other visitors looked on in horror. An armed sentry did not intervene in his defence, because bears were sacred to the town.

Murray's 1874 Guide to Switzerland gives a slightly different account when it says: 'In 1861 an English officer was destroyed by the large male bear, having fallen in a foolhardy attempt to pass along the wall separating two dens. The struggle was long, and took place in the presence of many witnesses.'

My father's mother also had a favourite son, whose name was Edgar. The sun shone from between his brows, as the saying goes, and he was the darling of the family, a slim and handsome young man whose fragile character was reflected in his wavering dark eyes.

When the Great War began in 1914 he foolishly enlisted with the army, but on discovering it to be nothing more than dysentery, haircuts, and barking dogs with human faces, he sensibly walked out of it, coming back to Nottingham one afternoon with a forlorn and bitter expression. His mother made him change into civilian clothes, and he was provided with a bicycle, food, some money, and a map, and sent to his sister Dolly who lived at Hinckley.

So that he would not get caught by the military police his father advised him to cycle along the tow-paths of the canals. Edgar and his brothers sat in the parlour with the map open and the curtains drawn plotting an escape route by the Trent-and-Mersey that would take him a good distance west before dipping to Burton-on-Trent. He had then to risk a seven-mile gap overland before getting back on to a canal which would twist its way through beautiful Leicestershire countryside to within a mile of his sister's place.

He left Nottingham at five in the morning and rode fast, making it by late suppertime, cock-a-hoop at his success. Stretching his legs across the hearth after a well-earned meal, he heard Dolly promise he could stay as long as he liked, for he was safe with her, though he must be careful not to visit pubs or show himself in the street. Glad to have her brother in the house, at the same time she was uneasy about shielding a deserter, though when it was a question of choosing between family and country there was no doubt what she would do.

Dolly and her husband bred dogs, and Eddie went to sleep cradled in the noise of their barking, which must have been a fair relief from the yapping he had recently escaped. A few days later he was recaptured in a pub and sent back to his battalion, where he was met with an increased renewal of it.

He deserted again, and once more came home for succour. The trail was hotter for him because the British Army was obscenely desperate for flesh, never having enough men to throw into the carnage of Belgium and north-eastern France.

Edgar hid in Robins Wood beyond the Cherry Orchard, and my fourteen-year-old father biked there every day to take his food. Edgar had pitched a tent and camouflaged it with leaves and branches. Sitting outside on a log he received dishes of hot pudding and meat, and cans of tea lovingly prepared by his mother.

But a cyclist policeman followed my father, and Edgar was caught once more. He was bundled straight off to France, and sent 'over the top' with the 7th Battalion of the Sherwood Foresters on the first day of the Battle of the Somme.

36

Out of love for the earth's surface, as fits somebody living in mists and deserts locked in a quest for the truth, I've always been fascinated by maps.

From as far back as I can remember I have felt inexorably drawn to printed representations of the earth's shape, to those delineations of the land's crust which have the achievements of civilisation stamped on them in the same sense that beautiful women of certain primitive tribes show off the elaborate designs etched on to their bodies. The first time I saw a map I wanted to leave home.

In planning a way by car from London to Leningrad, from Calais to Cordoba, or from Kiev to Venice – or from Harrogate to Haifa if we bring in the concept of the carferry – I enter the realm of mathematical vectors, though on the actual journeys I hardly consult the maps so that, drawn into the fluctuations of traffic and the unexpected exigencies of topography, it becomes anything but a constricting vacation.

Nothing interests me more – now as when I was a child – than to hear of a highway built where one had not existed before, or a new railway, or a shipping route opened through the ice, or a new town settled on the edge of sandy or forest wastes.

While anthropologists moan the ruination of primitive tribes when a motor road is laid along the mountain backbone of New Guinea, or the conservationists bewail another sky of fresh air polluted beyond redemption, I cannot deny my excitement at the empty quarters being amplified and re-created by man's endeavours, no matter how misguided this might seem in a more rational moment, just as at the same time I feel a sense of loss on hearing that deserts inexorably push their sand and barrenness into fertile oases.

In peering at maps of remote parts which lack the more intense communications of Europe and the United States, I wonder where new roads could be built for the exploitation of mineral resources. By prolonged attention I plan my own routes, but will not actually mark the map to make the new roads or railways appear more possible. Being spitted upon the truth I keep myself feeding on many worlds.

I also like obsolescent maps so as to see what the relief colours looked like without the roads which now go in bold red lines over mountain ranges and through forests. I compare sheet with sheet, and see that where the dotted lines of primitive trails were, is now a motor-road or a single track railway line. I imagine myself an engineer in charge of a new road, initiating surveys, sweating in a tent at dusk while glancing through the plans and elevations of another stage. I would draw them perhaps with the same attention to detail as my

90

lace-designer Uncle Frederick put into his intricate patterns before they were set up on the Nottingham machines.

It is as if maps existed before roads and railways were showered from space so that men would be able to set out for contiguous lands and get in touch with neighbouring tribes. The technological perfection of human maps has something magical about it. Whether the land is wild or tamed does not matter, but the links for cultural mixing and the construction of new towns make me feel safer on the earth, for it is a defence against nature and a means of sustaining civilisation.

But I also know that maps can be used as despicable instruments of oppression, for hunting and rounding up, for war and plunder. The civilisation they helped to create often counts its success by the number of its prisons, and it is difficult to imagine a new road being made without such buildings closer behind.

This conditional love of the earth's topography and its meticulous representation on paper leads me to wonder about the inner configuration of myself, a curiosity which falters because I know there is no fixed shape and texture of the inner man, no settled tectonic picture of the soul, no solid-and-drift in the layers of my skin.

Yet this acute comparison with the landscapes of the world is because the earth alone created the people who live on it, made man and all things out of soil and sea-water, moulded him by air and fire and liquid matter, moved him by fear and hunger and violence. He is and will always be at the mercy of what formed him, a multiplicity of components which, as far as searching among them for the truth is concerned, are beyond analysis.

And if emotional uncertainties are the only truths that the soul can possibly consist of, it will be a feverish and disordered map I shall finish with, that of a swamp as dangerous and untenable as where I began, perhaps even worse, for one is more likely to sink into spiritual extinction at the end of a search than at the time of setting out.

It often happens that, just before going away, I start to write a story, or even a novel. The stimulus of planning and the upset of preparation turns the senses in a creative direction, and I am prompted to tell something, though I rarely know what the end of it will be because I have to leave off and begin travelling.

The trip itself may be for no good reason except the muscle-flexing pleasure of moving on, but it cannot be denied when the veins are all set for it. It is no use protesting that whatever I wanted to say can wait till I come back, because it will never be the same again. The blood will be in a different spiritual zone, the maps around the feet redrawn, the heart and the eyes in another country.

The journey I am not a little beyond the middle point of is not the sort that takes me overland, but into the guts and around the darkness of the tripes. Myself, the earth, and time are indivisible during this peregrination, but the older I get the more it is necessary to scrape into the soil of time, even if it means digging the ground from under my feet so that I drop into the hole I have made.

The hole is in France. It is ten feet across and five feet deep. Edgar lies in it, rotting with terror though still sound in every limb, encompassed by the squalid rammel of the battle-field. Three corpses are on the anal tip of the crater, their khaki uniforms stained red and purple. Before falling into it Edgar saw them lying asleep in clumps and rows, some without legs and arms, all sinews ashen and shattered. Others were still screaming in horrible dreams: the sky was reality but they could not reach it.

Another man is wounded by a shrapnel bullet entering his stomach. He tries to spit out his shoulder-blades but they won't come loose, so he falls. Edgar has ammunition, but no rifle. The overcast sky is a vast and awful noise of bursting shells. The soil-and-chemical smell of explosions is as piercing as the sounds they make. It attacks another part of the senses. A massacre is taking place. Sixty thousand soldiers are being shot or blown to pieces for no reason at all, and Edgar wonders how as a human being he ever got into it.

37

The British Army has done for him – by hoping to move the battalion to which he belonged across a few inches of the 1 : 10,000 trench map – FONQUEVILLERS, SECOND EDITION, 57D N.E. SHEETS 1 & 2 (parts of) 1916.

His own officers, I heard him tell my father with a sort of crazed respect at their utter callousness, had lifted their revolvers to make sure the men went over the top. He remembered the voice petulantly barking as if they were cattle: 'Get on! Get on, then! Get on! Come on, you, get on. Get on, then. Get on!'

During their march to the battlefront, when the fields of northern France were in their most livid bloom, Edgar had been singled out by his battalion commander for a special talk because he had been a deserter. He was told that if there was any shirking of duty now that he was on active service he would be court-martialled for it and shot. To ram home the threat he was read a list of half a dozen names belonging to men who had so perished on that sector in the last month.

Two hundred and fifty of these heroes of common sense were murdered by their own firing-squads during the war, and many more were sentenced to long terms of imprisonment. Another way of dealing with 'criminals and troublemakers' was to form them into special 'Battle Patrols' and use them for the most dangerous enterprises.

The English war machine had spent nearly the whole of the nineteenth century limbering up for the super-butchery of the Great War. They tasted blood when Napoleon began his rampages, and had a go later in the Crimea, where thousands died. But the scores of minor colonial campaigns since then did not satisfy them, and they envied the Americans the slaughterous encounters of their Civil War. The great Henderson, who wrote so lovingly on Stonewall Jackson, theorised no end about it and regretted that the noble slave-owning south had lost.

Observers were sent to the Russo-Japanese War, which was studied in every detail, so that the Army Office in London could produce the most intricate maps and monographs. But not until 1914 did the military caste hone up their ineptness, and sniff the possibility of real home-brewed slaughter – or as near to home as they thought it reasonable to get.

38

In the diversionary attack at Gommecourt the 5th and 7th battalions of the Sherwood Foresters came out of their trenches, which were a foot deep in mud, and went towards the German lines.

During the week prior to the attack both battalions, like the rest of the 46th Division, had been continuously soaked to the skin, set in pouring rain at the hardest physical labour on trenches and earthworks. None of them had a night's sleep during this time, so that when they walked to their deaths on the morning in question, after a soldier's breakfast of a shit and a Woodbine, they were like men only half alive.

'Did you know,' Edgar began to my father one evening in a light-hearted mood, 'that there are three parts to an army? The vanguard up front, the rearguard behind, and the mudguard in the trenches – where I was!'

'I just went over the top with the others,' he continued in a more sombre tone, 'when the officer pointed his gun and shouted. None of us knew what we were doing. Or what to expect. We were all done in.'

Edgar went on to say that he was terrified, as afraid of his own officers and sergeants as of the German shellfire into which they walked, a fixation that put him in a state of mind in which he could only go forward dumbly.

He was not entirely empty of all except fear, however, for he sang, sometimes to himself, and then out loud as the gaps in the ranks were bigger, the ballad, 'To Be a Farmer's Boy' – which for some reason came back with sufficient insistence from his schoolboy days to keep him company during this dire accident of time.

In places the air became thick and yellow like a fog in winter, then it cleared to show a soldier younger than himself with a leg blown off. All green had gone from this short water-logged dip between the trenches, for it was now churned-up soil, clammy and pale, holed and fearful.

Somehow Edgar couldn't believe that shells and bullets were flying through the air; he thought that all this death was coming directly from the soil on which they stepped as they went forward, as if the very surface of the earth had turned into their mortal enemy.

If 8 August 1918, was, as Ludendorff said, the blackest day in the annals of the German Army (and there is no reason to disbelieve him, though it was even blacker in 1945), it is equally true that 1 July 1916, when Haig commenced his attack on the Somme, was a similarly dark day in the history of the British nation. Within ten minutes or so of the attack starting 60,000 men had fallen to the fire of a hundred German machine-gunners, and to their artillery. This is nearly as many casualties suffered by all sides during the whole day of the Battle of Waterloo.

'Still,' Edgar went on, 'we hadn't far to go. Not much more than a quarter of a mile between us and the Jerries, they said. Like trying to cross the Cherry Orchard from Colliers' Pad to Robins Wood. But we might as well have been trying to get at the moon.'

Laden with 70 pounds of equipment they clambered over the parapets and walked across no-man's land in parade-ground formation, a fact which all official and many unofficial histories mention with pride. The Germans who watched them advance under a cloudless sky and shot whole lines of them down spoke highly of their courage. It was a similar spectacle to when regiments of Zulus were launched against the rapid rifle fire of British infantry in the latter part of the 19th century – only this time it was the British themselves who fell in heaps. A seven-day bombardment before the attack had merely driven the Germans into their underground dugouts, some of which were forty feet deep and supplied with electric light, so that when on 1 July the bombardment stopped as a clear signal that the attack was about to begin, their machine-gunners rushed up to what remained of the parapets to meet the 'flower of British manhood'.

The British assault on the Somme was in fact an attack against part of a fortress and, bearing this in mind, it is illuminating to refer to a book called *Machine-gun Tactics* written by a Captain Applin seven years before. The tactics used (or not used) by the British on the Somme had failed even as far back as 1870–71, and again during the Japanese attack on the fortified zone of Port Arthur in 1904. As Applin so cogently wrote:

'When high explosive shells have destroyed the fortifications and disabled the artillery, the stormers will be met by rifle fire and that of machine-guns concealed among the ruins of the works. The intensity and accuracy of this fire will be such as to result frequently in the complete repulse of the assault, and even when the glacis of a work has been occupied it may be several weeks before the capture of the work itself is effected.'

But at half past seven on that Saturday morning, the British diversionary attack on the Somme at Gommecourt came across no-man's-land at a slow walk, the infantry having been led to believe that the guns had by this time smashed every living and resisting thing in their path, and that they more or less had only to stroll forward and 'take over' the German defences. In fact the walls of barbed wire had hardly been breached by millions of shells, which they discovered to their short-lived horror when they bunched up in hundreds at the few gaps open, and fell in heaps under the fire of the German gunners.

The French were quicker to grasp new tactical methods in regard to modern trench warfare. They did not obey their officers so blindly. On that part of the front where the British and French attacks made their junction, both armies went forward at zero hour. The French pushed over and across in small groups, fluid in movement and using all cover skilfully, a platoon the largest unit, dodging, dropping, springing up again – completely baffling the German artillery and machine-gunners – until they got to the opposing trenches and finished a successful attack.

But on their left were long lines of British infantry advancing slowly a few yards apart, coming up out of the trenches in wave after wave, dogged, determined, unimaginative, with complete trust in their officers, all with their own fears and thoughts, sent in perfect order to mangling and death.

Their long lines were clear and unmistakable targets, easy for artillery to range on, so that they were soon withering under clouds of exploding shells. The lines went north for twenty miles, and whole sections were inundated in earth and fire and smoke, trudging on through the pulverising flames of shot and shell.

The lines grew thin, but still went forward. Was this bravery, or were they cattle? They were butchered by machine-gunners, the lines getting thinner still, each man plodding over pitted and difficult ground until there was nothing left that looked like an army, and the culprits in command far behind were waiting in all their sodden stupidity for news of break-through and victory.

Those few who came back crawled across no-man's-land at dusk, after waiting in shell-holes all day. Edgar wasn't killed or wounded, and neither did he return to his own side. They would only have sent him on some other stunt, he said, which might really have killed him off, or he would have deserted on active service and got shot for it. With a dogged sort of insanity and courage he stayed in a shell-hole between the opposing trenches, hoping to surrender to the Germans as soon as it was possible.

He saw everything, without looking to the left or the right, or appearing to shift his eyes. No movement, nor any small thing out of place, escaped him. He seemed to have all-round vision, like a pigeon. But he said good-bye to the grey and turgid Trent near Gunthorpe, and the flat lush fields of Nottinghamshire. For a moment the soil smelt like beer, and then like blood.

Tortured by hunger and thirst, but above all fear, he many times wanted to go back to the comfort of his own unit, but was afraid that, being unwounded and without his rifle, he would be caught on a charge of desertion. Cries of dying and wounded surrounded him. On the attack across no-man's-land he had gone through rolls of wire as high as walls, and back through them again without knowing it.

In-and-out-the-window. I'll never send you where I wouldn't go myself, the colonel had said, but who cared for his promises now? Edgar did not know it, but the colonel who commanded his battalion had already been killed.

Enemy artillery and machine-guns ploughed and swept no-man's-land all day, to stop reinforcements reaching those few Foresters who had made a lodgement in the German trenches.

Just before dropping into the shell-hole Edgar was aware of a young officer, his arm hanging bloodily loose, running by him and shrieking in a voice he said he'd never forget till his dying day: 'Hopeless! Hopeless!'

Edgar saw how war was nothing more than fear, boredom, bullying and filth – all of them combining to create the lowest common denominator of life. War had sounded differently when read to them in stories at school, but he knew the truth of it now, as the officer with the shattered arm dropped with a bullet in his stomach.

He had collapsed through total exhaustion, and nobody bothered him because they were too intent on trying to save themselves, though few of them did. He did not know how long he lay in the crater, nor could he remember being picked up by the Germans, but after what seemed years during that Saturday night (and Sunday morning) of his soul he found himself sitting in one of their trenches, and recalled that they had treated him kindly. As he sat on a wooden box with a mug of German coffee about to touch his lips he remembered where he had last heard 'To Be a Farmer's Boy'. A couple of weeks ago, at a concert party 'somewhere in France', he had joined in the chorus, momentarily full of joy.

When a German aeroplane on a mission of mercy and

courtesy flew over the British front on July 4th and dropped a list of wounded and unwounded prisoners that their side had taken, Edgar's name was on it.

Both battalions of Sherwood Foresters were wiped out in this diversionary attack. No gains were expected, and none were made. Blinds were drawn in every Nottingham street, for the battalions had suffered over 1,200 casualties on this small sector, and another Forester battalion lost 500 men further south. The only small advance was on the extreme right of the twenty-mile front where British troops, attacking in co-operation with the French left, had the assistance of their more efficient artillery.

The 'disappointing performance' of the 46th (North Midlands) Division, of which the 5th and 7th Battalions Sherwood Foresters were a part, caused it to be kept out of all important battles from then on – except for an assault against the Hindenburg Line in 1918, during the last Hundred Days of the War. At Gommecourt they were thought to have let down their London-Scottish comrades of the 56th Division attacking the south side of the salient, who got further in to the German lines.

When officers of the 8th Battalion Sherwood Foresters stood – eight months later – on some of the German concrete machine-gun emplacements at Gommecourt opposite the British trenches of July 1st 1916 they saw what a magnificent field of fire the Germans had had. They also saw lines of dead bodies from that tragic day still lying in no-man's-land.

The British staff considered July 1st a success because the New Armies, over which so much care was said to have been taken, had stood up well under fire. In other words, they had died rather than run away, perished rather than improvise, though some officers were to complain afterwards how difficult and at times impossible it had been to get men who had been designated to carry wire into no-man's-land to form up and become part of an attacking wave.

The assault might have proved more successful if they had been taught to stay alive – as all good soldiers should be – if they had dashed across at night, for example, with no equipment except a shovel and a few grenades, which would have achieved just as much, if not a great deal more. At such a time the British Army should have called on a nation of poachers instead of a nation of cricketers. It was war, not sport, but the casualty list on this day or perhaps at some other time might have included the following group of names – though it was never sure whether they were killed, wounded, or simply missing:

L/Cpt John Cade	7th Buffs
Pte Robert Hood	11th Sherwood Foresters
Pte Robert Kett	8th Norfolk
Pte Edward Ludd	5th Sherwood Foresters
Sgt William Posters	7th Sherwood Foresters
Pte Thomas Straw	London Rifle Brigade
Cpt George Swing	7th Royal West Kent
Pte Richard Turpin	1st Essex
Cpl Walter Tyler	2nd Essex

Their demise was not reported in *The Times*, though in their disappearance they were not divided.

39

Reading the Official Histories of the Battle of the Somme, one is struck by the vast preparations that went on for months beforehand, of the immense labour of building roads, tramways and narrow-guage railways through the otherwise empty fields, and the erecting of tents, depots and huts; the hauling of ammunition and guns, the sinking of wells for water, the siting and equipping of hospitals to receive the wounded, the allotting of so many trains per division for its supplies – all this meticulous timetable planning to create a superb and efficient factory for getting 300,000 men up to the front and into slaughter, an organisation that covered the whole of northeastern France. The only trouble was that it didn't work.

There were nearly a million and a half British soldiers in France and Belgium on 30 June 1916, holding ninety miles of front, making an average of ten men of all arms to defend every yard of ground facing the Germans. On most sectors of the line this was much less, since the proportion of those parts where an offensive was being prepared – e.g. the Somme – had to be more or less double.

A linear city in which fighting almost never ceased during four years stretched from the English Channel to the Swiss frontier. Some four million men on either side had to be provided with food, water, clothing, guns and ammunition, as well as other impedimenta and necessities of ordinary life. It was Slaughter City stretched out over the fields for 400 miles, ammunition wagons going one way, ambulances the other – the same on both sides.

All the so-called civilised and intellectual brains of Europe were engaged in trying to discover ways of breaking into the other half of this composite city of mud trenches, strongpoints, dugouts, tents, huts, and, further back, real houses and halls in towns and villages. Where the two civilisations met it was a waste-ground, a blood-soaked rammel-tip, a shanty-town of bones and death, a vast fearful stinking serpentine conglomeration of misdirected energy and talent which has since been commemorated as something glorious in thousands of shabby poppy-strewn pre-totalitarian war memorials up and down the country, and in every country in Europe.

40

After the opening of the Somme battle it was plain that the British people were willing to accept the appalling casualties of their soldiers, and that the soldiers themselves would take whatever massacres were foisted on them by the incompetents

101

in control. Such passive attitudes allowed the offensive to continue, and led to the Passchendaele carnage of the following year. No great voice was lifted against this internal ripping to pieces of a country.

The British were all right as long as they did the attacking and were being shot down or blown to pieces. It was as if casualties actually kept up their morale – at least one is led to believe so by those who did not do the fighting. It was the staff officers' war. They stayed alive, and as such the war belonged to them. Those officers who did die perished willingly in the public school spirit. For the old men in command it was a game of tactics in which live pieces were used, though it soon degenerated into a penny dreadful for those other ranks who in their gloom and despair did not know how to end it except by getting killed themselves.

On the Somme the strongest part of the German line was selected for attack. For this reason the Germans doubted that it would after all be made there, in spite of the preparations. The clues that it might be the spot chosen could be seen as a feint, so the British prided themselves on having achieved strategical surprise, a useless advantage when the defences are impregnable. But the Germans held themselves ready, in case it should after all turn out to be the real thing.

The British commanders did not know how to keep the times of their attacks secret, as if the more dead and wounded lying between the lines, the more successful the battle. There was no such thing as surprise, not only because of lengthy bombardments which advertised an attack loud and clear for days if not weeks beforehand but because it was always possible to trick the exact date of the offensive out of the British Army staff.

The French would not unreasonably want to know when their villages were going to be in danger from artillery retaliation and counter-attack. But at the same time there may have been someone among them able to transmit information across to the Germans.

Despite the so-called impregnable defences that each front line presented to the other, enterprising civilians did occasionally find it possible to cross from occupied into unoccupied territory, and vice versa. The French authorities admitted that they were never able to prevent this traffic.

The British staff, scornful of petty secrecy, were dangerous romantics who had never heard of spies. In any case, British grit was always supposed to triumph in the end, in spite of corpse-filled shell-holes, or bodies hanging like scarecrows on the barbed wire to rot in full view of eighteen-year-olds who had not yet 'gone over the top' but were soon to do so.

In February 1916 the inhabitants of Meaulte, close to the Somme and behind the front line, were ordered to evacuate their village, since they would be in peril when the big attack started. But the inhabitants did not want to leave, in spite of the danger, protesting that they would not only lose their livestock but, more important, the whole of the present year's crop.

They sent an eloquent and moving petition to King George V in London, explaining their feelings on the matter. One of the king's secretaries passed it back to Sir Douglas Haig, the British Commander in France, who had the magnanimity to allow the French villagers to stay where they were, warning them however that they must remain in their houses for *three days from 1 July*. Months in advance, therefore, he had given away the exact date of the British attack. From then on the Germans began to strengthen their line which, even after 400,000 casualties and five months later, the British failed to break.

Yet on the first day of the Somme battle the British Army was at the height of its quality regarding the skill and spirit of the men. This was never to be regained, at any time during the rest of the war. It was wasted away in ten minutes. Though the soldiers of the Somme were only half-trained compared to the pre-war peacetime army, they could fire their rifles generally at a more rapid rate than those who came later. As volunteers they possessed 'dash' and intelligence, while those conscripts of the next two years became dogged and despairing, and tried to stay alive longer, though they had little chance of doing so. It was admitted by the staff that they did not have the quality of the men who went down on the Somme.

The blow finished Britain as a world power, and as a

country fit for any hero to live in. The heroes and their heroic spirit were dead. If they had survived they would indeed have insisted after the war that England be made habitable for them. But such an insistence would have disturbed the old order too fundamentally for its comfort, which with sadistic prescience saw to it therefore that those heroes did not outlast them.

The men of the Somme did not die because they wanted to perpetuate the class structure of English cities and the English countryside, nor the power of those five per cent who owned ninety-five per cent of the country's wealth. As they went up to the front they thought some unwritten and unspoken agreement existed that this would be done away with for ever if they took part with all their might and main in the war.

They did not fight for England *as it was*. They fought to *change* England, as much as, if not more than, to protect their country from the Germans with whom, deep down, they had no quarrel. The fact is that their deaths (which they did not expect) only made sure that the England they disliked would remain in the ascendant. In that sense they actually betrayed their country by going to fight for it. But it is difficult not to succumb to treachery when it is callous enough.

41

At Messines Ridge on 7 June 1917, nearly a year after the first Somme battle, the British Army tried again. It blew up the German front line, and moved forward over the earthquake zone which had been created. Nine divisions (about 80,000 men) took part in the attack, with three more divisions in support.

'Briefly,' says the army manual on demolitions and mining, 'the tendency of low explosives is to shift, and of high explosives to shatter.' I did not know this when I read of the Messines assault, or when my father gloated over the sudden skyward direction of the Hill 60 part of the ridge.

Tunnels were dug under the German trenches, and 19 loads of ammonal were stacked in their secret places. Ammonal is a slightly sticky substance like damp sugar. One might say that it is crystalline and doesn't flow very well, and that though it is fairly dry it has to be kept from getting wet. For this reason it is packed in hermetically sealed tins, which must be placed close together so that detonation waves will pass through and ignite the well-tamped cache. A detonator and primer is buried in the charge. Ammonal produces a lifting effect, and so is ideal for mined charges.

Nearly a million pounds of it – over 400 tons – were made ready for the attack, so packed that, after ignition, its force would go only upwards. There were 55 tons alone under Hill 60, the unsuspecting Germans snug in their bunkers above. When the 1,000,000 pounds went off at dawn the whole sky was . . . but the dreadful picture has been many times described.

There was enough shattered flesh on the pulverised landscape of Messines and its Ridge to satisfy even Alegabalus of Rome – or Heliogabalus, if one hasn't read Burton on boozing, melancholy and bellicose wrath.

As someone said who 'went through it': 'There were bodies all over the place – but what a state they were in. They were so ripped up you'd have needed a sewing machine to stitch them back together again. But they were too far gone for that.' Four mines to the south-east of Ploegsteert Wood were not exploded at zero hour during a later stage of the battle, because the position had already been evacuated. It was intended to remove this quantity of more than 100,000 lbs of explosive after the war, but the matter was overlooked, and the charges are still in position today.

Burrowing by British soldier-miners and uniformed navvies had been going on for eighteen months. The longest tunnel was over 700 yards, the deepest more than 100 feet. Many of the explosions had a radius of destruction of 200 feet. Thousands of German soldiers were killed. Many went mad. Thousands more were taken prisoner.

And one more ridge was captured.

42

The explosions did their job. The dawn attack was successful. But though open land lay before the troops quite early in the morning they were paralysed by the vacillations of the inexperienced staff who examined maps with glazed eyes miles away in comfortable chateaux and manor houses.

If the men were unable to exploit what they had bravely and painfully won — for the earthquake landscape still had to be fought over — it wasn't entirely for lack of ability at bringing up reserves. Often they were immediately to hand, but the staff were crushed by the problem of moving them. They had not planned to break through, therefore when they did it was not exploited.

Instead of advancing down the valleys on the other side of the ridge and throwing the German front into confusion by capturing Comines, the troops on their hard-won high ground, tired after the fighting and happy that they had survived, took off their tunics and lay in the sunshine because no one could tell them what to do, until the returning Germans began to pick them off in dozens, finding good targets in their white skins.

The Messines attack, begun with such brilliancy and hope, fizzled miserably out. Casualties were unexpectedly light at first, but then mounted rapidly with the confusion and incompetence to a total of over 24,000 — half of whom were from the Anzac Division. As has often been said before, and cannot be repeated too many times, the Germans considered that the British soldiers fought like lions, but were led by donkeys.

The gaps were occasionally there for the infantry to go forward, but the yeomen farmers and country gentlemen in uniform had the antique vision of galloping through on their horses to finish off the Germans with swords and lances! They couldn't leave such 'glory' to the lower-class craftsmen and clerks and slum-dwellers. The élite of the army, the cavalry, must have its turn. They waited impatiently on their fine horses, cursing the infantry because they had not cut the wire properly, and the artillery for making so many holes on the ground that their horses would be held up, and their spotless tunics splashed with mud.

But the infantry made a big mistake when they broke open the German defences. They did not carry with them boxes of live foxes, to be released at the right moment so that the fox-hunting cavalry commanders champing in the fields behind could begin a wild, tally-hoing, unstoppable chase. If the foxes had been sturdy and resourceful the foxhunters might have made it to the Rhine before the baffled German reserves had collected their wits and closed in, and driven them into the water.

Certainly the British infantry would have been glad to see them go, while those who were not could have followed them. Of the rest, the pigeon-fanciers might have sent back racers telling of the famous victory, and the ex-colliers celebrated with whippet races, while those still bored and unconvinced could have finished off the corpse-eating rats in no-man's-land – a combination of animal scenes worthy of the great Doctor Doolittle himself.

43

For every officer killed or wounded on the first day of the Battle of the Somme, twenty-two other ranks fell with him. During the whole of the Boer War, in which the total British casualties were under 17,000, the proportion was one officer to eleven other-ranks.

If Waterloo was won on the playing fields of Eton, the British class war was fought out on the Western Front with real shells and bullets. The old men of the upper classes won by throwing the best possible material into the slaughter, including their own high-spirited and idealistic young. But the masses who joined up were people who had been perfected by more than a century of the Industrial Revolution. In one sense they were indeed the flower of mankind: intelligent, technically minded, and literate, men of a sensibility whose loss sent England as a country into a long decline. When they died, as nearly a million did, they took their skills with them.

Such people were thrown away with prodigal distaste because they were coming to the point of stepping into their own birthright. Their potential was about to become manifest, and they would have demanded what had been denied them for so long. War seemed the only alternative to revolution, and the leaders of every nation were faced by the same cosmic problem.

They sided with destiny and chose war, but by the end of it revolution had come in any case, and the exhausted peace or truce soon brought in another round of war and revolution that began in 1939 and has by no means ended yet. Wars can be started, but revolutions can never be stopped, for whoever creates war makes revolution, which then seems the surest chance of winning peace, even after the longest of wars. 'Only revolution can save the earth from hell's pollution,' said Byron, though one cannot believe that in their heart of hearts those key men of 1914 thought exactly that. Time goes more slowly than we think. The Great War has ended, but Europe is only now recovering.

To go back to the trenches is but a small step, and no one yet knows the true meaning of what went on there. The men of 1914 were slaughtered, and indeed allowed themselves to be slaughtered – which was the fatal flaw in their perfectability. The old men of the upper classes who were in command possessed the half-concealed knowledge that if they did not dispose of them in this sporting roulette-wheel fashion then those millions would turn round and sweep them away.

It was perhaps the last viciously competent task that the British upper class was to perform, and it is from the Great War that the drift between officers and men, governing and governed, between those lavish with the blood of others, and those frugal with the rich life they saw themselves on the point of beginning to enjoy, really began. Before 1914 a unity could have been possible, and the men might have tried it. Joining up to fight was, in a sense, their way of saying yes, but the old men used this affirmation to try and finish them off.

In order to maintain a mythical 'balance of power' on the mainland of Europe, or to arse-lick over the humanly meaningless alliances concocted in some cosy office or dreamlike court, they destroyed the internal balance of the country. England was an imperial power that embarked on a war of aggressive defence. When there were no more colonies left to grab, the empires of the world went for each other's throats. Germany tore the guts out of the British Empire, and choked on them.

The best that can be said is that the upper classes lacked the imagination to realise what they were doing, though their subconscious must have known well enough. Never before had such an assault been made of class against class, and the music of the German machine-guns and the percussion of their artillery on the Somme must have caused some ambiguous emotions in those who sent the men over, except that many heard the music from a distance, if at all.

For four years British soldiers were slung against the impregnable German defences, flesh against flying steel, and they never really succeeded in breaking through. The army did so in 1918 only because the Americans had started to bring their fresh skill and material into the war.

The nearest the British came to it was at Cambrai in 1917. This was due to the technical knowledge and the calm tenacity and bravery of the men in 400 tanks. They laid the German defences wide open, but the staff was so tragically incompetent that even with an armoured force that no one had ever seen before, and against which the Germans had as yet little defence, they could not take advantage of the silent and empty road leading into the abandoned city of Cambrai. They could not believe their luck and so, as always in such cases, luck continued to run against them. The other breakages of the German front, on the Somme on 14 July 1916, later the same year at Flers, and at Third Ypres the following year could not be exploited because there were no live men left to push through the gaps.

But if the British had finally succeeded in breaking through, the staff would have sent the army into a disaster far greater than that of a failed attack. With patient, maladroit negligence they would have concocted humiliation as well as tragedy for the men. Something in their bone-heads must have warned them of the dangers in pushing on when the gap was opened, of getting a few divisions through into open country where they would be at the mercy of quick-moving German reserves, to be surrounded and hammered into annihilation. The army would lose so many men that they would be in no position to play at war with them much longer. The higher echelons of the staff might then have their own bodies threatened by shot and shell, and that was never their idea at all.

44

Too high a standard was set for the men in the line by officers who never went near it. The front was regarded by the General Staff as a temporary fixture which was liable to alter at any time, for when the big push came and the breakthrough happened, no more trenches would be needed because the troops would lead the staff in a fine dash towards Potsdam. And it was liable to come at any minute, for one never knew when the Germans would crack.

Consequently, the British trenches were rarely allowed to become too comfortable for fear the soldiers would get soft, or that they wouldn't want to leave them when told to get up and attack the Germans. They must never be corrupted by the defensive spirit while one more useless sacrifice could be wrung from them. In 1917 the Russian Army voted with its feet for peace by getting out of the line as fast as it could. The British Army on the Somme and at Passchendaele voted with its corpses for death.

When Lloyd George asked General Pétain what his opinion

was of the costly and fruitless attacks of the British Army in Flanders he was told: 'You can't fight the Germans and the mud at the same time.'

Pétain was equally forthright when asked whether the British attacks had assisted the French Army to recover from its mutinies in 1917. 'Your attacks did help us,' he admitted, 'but they ruined the British Army.'

The British Staff must have been a preening, self-conscious lot, and imagined every soldier to be the same, for they made sure their positions were always overlooked by the Germans. They liked being chiked at from hilltop and ridges. All along the front, from the high dunes of the Belgian seacoast, south via the hills near Ypres, the Messines Ridge, Vimy Ridge, and the uplands before Bapaume, it was indeed a theatre of war to the Germans, who were invariably permitted by the gallant British staff to have the best seats in it.

The British Army was used as a battering ram against an unbreakable door. The soldiers who formed it looked bitterly at high ground up which they would have to advance. Every year of the war they were led out on an annual bloodbath, and though the door of the German defences creaked and cracked, it never burst open.

In spite of the French troubles at Verdun, the British should not have attacked for at least another two years, so that the New Army could have been trained to the standard of its opponents and, more important, so that its officers could have been properly instructed. The German war machine, dangerous as it was, could have been slowly bled to death by the many allies, instead of being continually and suicidally attacked.

At the beginning, in 1914, one could say that as the 'moral' to the physical is three to one, so the German attacker (as always with the attacker who has the 'moral' on his side) had a twenty to one advantage over the defender. But since the defender was not immediately defeated, and his forces after the German defeat at the first battle of the Marne in September 1914 gradually began to outnumber those of the attacker, then that attacker could eventually have been bled to death. Thus the original advantage of the attacker's onslaught became a terrible drain on the world. After the German retreat from the

Marne they hinted that they were ready to end the fight, but the French said: 'First give us back our dead.'

The British Army should have gone on to the defensive in the spring of 1915, and its government at the same time tried to make peace. The Germans might not have accepted the terms of withdrawal to their own frontiers at that time, but perhaps after two more years of stalemate they might have seen it as the only possible course.

Robert Graves, in his essay 'The Kaiser's War' (from his book *Difficult Questions, Easy Answers*) suggests, with good reason 'that the Entente leaders should have negotiated for peace in 1916, when invited by President Wilson and the Pope, and urged by Lord Lansdowne; and when the Emperor of Austria and the Kaiser were both ready to treat.'

Though neither side could win, the British generals believed (and the Germans to a certain extent still hoped) that time would throw up some solution. Thus the manhood of many nations was used in a diabolical war of attrition.

The British Command maintained its ludicrous faith in the suicidal maxim that the best defence lies in the attack – which it may, but only if you can be sure of winning. Otherwise it leads to frustration, reaction, and stubbornness – this latter a fatal quality in the British character when it is given a free run, for it crushes fresh thought, destroys flexibility, and scoffs at improvisation. It is, fatally, too often considered a fair substitute for energy. Its moral worth, though of great value, is ruined by lack of creative evaluation.

More than two years were to go by before Lieutenant-General Sir John Monash showed how an attack could be made without incurring massive casualties – in the offensive before Amiens by the Australians and Canadians on 8 August 1918. Monash, if any man can be singled out for such an honour, was the person responsible for Ludendorff's cry that 'the 8th of August was the blackest day of the German Army in the history of the war.' A few more generals with the intellect of Monash might have saved the British Army hundreds of thousands of dead and cripples, and brought some kind of victory to it as well. But such people were rare, and the fools and criminals were too many.

An engineer by profession, Monash was both original and intelligent; but most of all, he was thorough. In his appreciation of the problems confronting him he did not seem beset by that evil genius of the English which Robert Burton defined as 'idleness'.

He made his men train in combination with the actual tank crews before they went into battle together. When the attack opened and his men moved forward he arranged for ammunition to be dropped by parachute. The artillery barrage was only to begin on the day of the attack, and not a week before.

It was as if the longer the casualty lists became, the closer the staff must have thought they were to wearing down the Germans, and to victory. It never came in the sense they sought it, not finally until 1945, when the Bolshevism they loathed had had twenty-five years to stiffen (or terrify) the Russian character which was said in 1917 to have let the Allies down so badly. The Germans were finally finished off as a military nation at Stalingrad and Kursk.

The scene of the earth's bloodletting had shifted to those places in Russia, where it might easily have come to the close infighting country of south-east England and the great slum jungles of urban London.

But perhaps Hitler baulked at invading England in 1940 because he knew from personal experience that he could expect a fight to the finish, or at least another terrible ding-dong bloodbath such as frequently took place in Belgium and Flanders during the Great War between British and German troops.

As a member of a Bavarian regiment – (were all Prince Rupprecht's Bavarian regiments set against the British Army because their country had been put to fire and sword by the Duke of Marlborough's troops in 1704? Or because they had once been Napoleon's allies and couldn't be trusted against the French?) – as a member of a Bavarian regiment Hitler, that stunted company runner with his obsession against all human beings, seems always to have been on parts of the front opposite the British.

At the First Battle of Ypres in 1914 his regiment was reduced from 3,500 men to less than 600 in attacks against the Black Watch and the Coldstream Guards. He had a long memory where his own body had been injured – and so he might well have hesitated against the English, at least until he had finished Russia, which he never did.

The British battalion commanders in the First World War did not like the uncomfortable mud, but death and replacements made them feel they were actually getting somewhere. Raids and minor attacks were constantly launched, ostensibly to keep up the spirits of their men and foster the tigerish grit of aggression in them. But as soon as they had to stop much of this, in the eerie winter of 1917-1918, and go on the defensive because they really had no more men to throw away, the Germans came back and broke through with comparative ease, on 21 March 1918.

Haig, Britain's number one war criminal, expected the Germans to advance in this attack at the same slow pace of his own clumsily-planned assaults. The remnants of the Fifth Army were hardly able to save themselves because it had been insisted that the British soldiers should have no training in the art of retreat. By this time the army was so weakened in morale that it could not be trusted to do it properly. If it couldn't attack, then it had to fight and die where it stood.

This senseless edict took away their chance of life, for tens of thousands were killed. In actual fact the British Army excelled in the art of retreat – as in the fighting withdrawal of 136 miles in thirteen days from Mons in 1914, when the small British Expeditionary Force faced several German Army corps which attempted to envelop and destroy it.

With encouragement and planning a similar operation might have been repeated in 1918, but there was panic and rout in what was left of the Fifth Army as it fell back – with the usual acts of great and unquestionable bravery. Discipline cracked, and only the French divisions, recently recovered from their own mutinies, saved the British from disaster. Even so, trouble occasionally broke out in the British Army. In September 1917 there was a mutiny at the Etaples Base Camp which needed two battalions from the Front to put it down.

In the March retreat of 1918 brute force was used to bring

the soldiers to heel. Redcaps and officers held gangs of stragglers at gunpoint to herd them back into the fight. Not all casualties were caused by the Germans. The full story of the retreat has yet to be written, though it probably never will be. Many old scores were settled in the confusion. Men shot their own officers and sergeant-majors with more readiness than usual – though one heard of this happening during the rest of the war as well, such frequent tales that there must have been some truth in them.

After this defeat of 22 March 1918 the King was decorating a soldier of the 2nd Battalion Sherwood Foresters who had been in the unit since the beginning of the war. 'You must have seen some hard fighting in your time,' the King remarked. 'Yes, sir,' the soldier replied, 'but this last was the bloody limit!!'

Later in the year when the British were constantly attacking – and advancing – they were temporarily halted at what was called the Beaurevoir Line. There were still fairly heavy casualties in this last Hundred Days of the war, and the Tommy's irrepressible but grim humour led him to call it the 'au revoir' line.

45

There was, of course, the affair of Meteren, which took place in the afternoon of 14 April 1918.

I have scoured official histories, and searched divisional accounts, but can find no mention of it save in one book: *Machine Guns: Their History and Tactical Employment* – being also a history of the machine gun corps, 1916–1922 – by Lieutenant-Colonel G. S. Hutchinson, published in 1938.

In the German offensive on the Lys, which began on the 9th of April, the Portuguese Corps had disintegrated and the British were routed. The great German artillery train of heavy guns had moved north from the Somme, and Bruchmuller's music of hell began pounding away to their subtle and sadistic fire-plan.

The front caved in. Men ran, the only sensible course. They 'panicked' – that official and libellous word for self-preservation.

Many soldiers were young and inexperienced, and the retreat was fast, the demoralisation widespread. It seemed for a while as if they would not stop till they reached the Channel, either to be taken prisoner, or lifted off by the navy.

Higher ranks tried to stop the rout, but many officers were simply running with their men, and refused to halt and turn round to the enemy even when ordered.

A picture of the collapse is given by the aforementioned Colonel Hutchinson, who commanded the Machine Gun Battalion of the 33rd Division – which was ordered to the village of Meteren, near Bailleul, to defend a hill of great tactical importance.

He relates how on his reconnaisance, on 12 April, he went into a roadside *estaminet* and found a crowd of British stragglers, fighting drunk. He ordered a machine gun to be trained on them, and sent them forward, towards the Germans where, he said 'they perished to a man.'

By 14 April the Germans were attacking once more, and again men were inclined to flee. The commander of the Machine Gun Battalion therefore ordered the sergeants in charge of the gun teams to fire on any British troops who began to retreat. He then goes on to say how 'from near the mill I saw one of my gunners destroy a platoon of one regiment which in its panic had taken to flight.'

For this confession of atrocity no one was ever brought to trial. The line at this point had only recently been reinforced by very young and half-trained soldiers, boys mostly who were dragged unwilling from farm and factory, slum and office. For not playing the game, and obeying the stringent rules laid down for them, the Gestapo machine-gunning officers and sergeants murdered them.

As far as I can ascertain from the Official History the units from which the forty murdered men of this platoon could have come were the 1st Scottish Rifles, the 1st Queen's Regiment, the XII Corps Reinforcement Battalion, or from three platoons of the 8th Middlesex (Pioneers). Owing to the confusion of the retreat, in which so many units were engaged, it is difficult to be more explicit. A rout is confusion: all the neat battalion records of set piece trench-to-trench attacks break down.

But if anyone lost a member of his family on this day and from one of those regiments it is possible that they were not shot by the Germans, but that they were butchered when faced with an overdose of British rancour.

How many more were there?

46

Let us continue with another question. Who *was* Lt/Col Graham Seton Hutchinson? A few bare facts can be obtained. He was born in 1890, and was commissioned in the King's Own Scottish Borderers in 1909. He served in Egypt, the Sudan and India. In 1914 he was in the 93rd Gordon Highlanders (he was proud of his Scottish ancestry) and later commanded (as we know) the 33rd Battalion of the Machine Gun Corps. His war record was distinguished in that he won the Military Cross, was awarded the Distinguished Service Order, was wounded three times, and mentioned in despatches four times – a common enough tale in those years.

Just after the Great War he was involved in political work in Poland, and it was here that he seems to have become infected with the virulent anti-semitism which lasted till his death. He was a writer of sorts, and considered himself a landscape painter also. Some sixteen books, mostly on military and 'political' topics, were written under his own name. A similar number (many of them trashy adventure novels on the Sexton Blake level, with Jews or foreigners as villains) came out under the pseudonym 'Graham Seton'. '*The Governor of*

Kattowitz was one such anti-semitic yarn, published in 1930.

Some of the non-fiction volumes were even more rabid. One such was in unashamed praise of Nazi Germany. He formed the NATIONAL WORKERS MOVEMENT in England in 1933, taking as his model the various organisations he had visited in Nazi Germany. He was on the Executive Council of the National Playing Fields Association, and also on the Executive Committee of Gordon Boys School. His favourite pastime was the cultivation of delphiniums. During the Second World War he worked for the Air Ministry, and died in 1946.

47

Most of those who came back from the Great War did not want to talk about their experiences, were embarrassed if one questioned them, became furtive in their recollections, as if they had taken part in something shameful.

It was left to the self-confident, extrovert, unimaginative commanding officers to arrange for the military histories of their units to be written, perhaps in order to wipe away some of the shame that they might otherwise have felt. Men I spoke to in childhood were savagely wry: 'Never again. They only sent us to France because they wanted to get us killed.' Not for them the regimental histories, to pore over with their hearts that had been steeped in the bitter realism of war. If they could have bothered with any reminiscences at all they might have preferred the highlighted accounts of disillusioned poets who were, after all, humanly closer to them.

They were sour and sad because they had been dragged into war by the foetid, super-efficient ruling-class machine that for a thousand years had perfected its grip on their souls – but which did not know how to win a war when it came to fighting one, or how to stop it when the blood-bill ran too high. And the men were angrier at the fact that they had allowed themselves to be betrayed, final proof that their manhood had gone and, with it, that supreme self-confidence which had only become apparent to them when they had already offered themselves up to the war, by which time it was too late.

To give the impression, as history books do, that the British nation volunteered for the war 'as one man' is false. Perhaps one man can do so. After one man, another will follow, and even if the time gap is infinitesimal, it cannot be said that they went to the recruiting centres together – though it was to the advantage of government propagandists to have the population believe that this was so. I would like to think that one followed another like sheep, or that a hundred men were paid by the War Office to stand outside a recruiting centre and have their photographs taken, than that they sprang to it like automatons.

All sorts of tricks and pressures were employed to get men into the army in the two years before conscription came. Those of a certain class who did not hurry to join up finally capitulated when nanny met them in the street and handed them a white feather for cowardice. My Uncle Frederick, who said that this became quite common, was offered one on the top deck of a tram by an elderly woman. Instead of blushing with shame he gave her a violent push: 'Leave me alone, you filthy-minded old butcher!'

Then he made his way off the tram expecting to be pursued by howls of 'universal execration' from other passengers, but they were embarrassed and silent, so that he walked down the steps unmolested.

This nanny appeared to have mistaken him for some type which he clearly was not. They seemed determined, he told me, to get their revenge on those young gentlemen whom they had been forced to spoil and mollycoddle as infants. They also possessed more than a residue of spite against the parents they had been bullied by, and retaliated now by hurrying their pet sons into the trenches – or any sons they could get their hands on, for that matter. It was one more example, he added, of how war puts the final touch of degredation on certain people in whom it has already got a fair grip. Not that this was meant to malign the women. Far from it. Men did the fighting, after all.

119

In war it is the worst of a country that persuades the best men to die. It is easier to deceive the best than the worst. But if it is true that the best men are fools and go with ease, while the worst are cunning and find it easy to hold back, what else can war be but an utterly sure method of destroying a country? Uncle Frederick argued against this, and said that any who went deserved exactly what they got. I was inclined to take his word for it, for he himself never put on any uniform, and so bolstered my faith in humanity.

He thought it was a case of the old wanting their revenge against the young. Those young men who fight and come back will then grow up to revere the values of the old who made sure they went – so the old in their deadly wisdom fondly imagine. And who can say they are wrong? The geriatrics stay behind to cheer them on, while the less senile put their black-hearted experience into smoothing out the paths that lead to the splintered sinews and dereliction of the battlefield.

One does not want to be unjust to those who took part in the war, but I do not see why the dead need war memorials, since they are already dead and so have no more requirements of this world. Perhaps the living want them more, to try and justify the feeling of guilt they have towards the dead, the guilt that eats at the living because they survived. No dishonour is done to the dead by wanting to see all war memorials destroyed. As for survivors still sound in wind and limb, they wouldn't want them either if they hadn't been worked on to desire them by those self-same people who manipulated their sentiments and got them into the war in the first place.

What about the maimed, blind, gassed, and limbless who, after all, paid the most? The only real voice they have left is that which enables them to cry out now and again for a living pension or pittance with which to sustain themselves. I feel sure that, knowing what it is to be maimed for a lifetime, they would not go into that war or any if they could have their lives over again.

One might say, in ranting against the awful waste and slaughter, that the officers and members of the government, the priests, scholars, and authors who promoted the enterprise, are no longer alive and here to listen, so why shout? And if they were, it would make no difference, because they would not hear.

Yet people exactly like them are still here today and would do the same again – conditions permitting – in different ways, using other means, if given the chance. Every time it happens it seems as if it has never happened before. The same people are still either crushing or perverting the people. One must resist all authority, regimentation, law, and dehumanising sameness – whether it comes from a government itself, or the backside of its soul called the silent majority. One can never say: 'All that sort of thing is finished' – because nothing is ever finished without eternal vigilance and united action when the ugly head of unthinking patriotism is raised.

Only Blonk, who married Edith, had varied feelings about the war. I got the gist of this when he was telling one of his sons about his time as a gunner in the Ypres Salient:

'We should have torn their fucking guts out for that fucking million dead, even if it cost us another million. We was all rearing to go in 1918, but the fuckers got an armistice. The fucking high-ups started the war, and when we got the Jerries on the run, they made us stop. We should have gone all the way into Germany and blown the fucking place sky-high, we should. They wouldn't have fucking-well started again in such a hurry under that fucking Hitler.'

He always said he'd never lift another finger for *them*, but in 1940 he went into the Home Guard, being still in his middle forties, and stronger than many an ordinary soldier – though some said he only went in for the overcoat and boot allowance.

'As long as there's no mud,' he said, 'I'll go to bloody hell and back. But mud – I detest it. Seen too many of my mates drowned in it when we was running the guns up to Passchendaele. 'Orses as well. It stank like boggery!'

Then he'd change into his sergeant's uniform, and go with grim-set face to put the others of his platoon through their paces.

48

The loud voices of the birds told me it would soon be light, but I hadn't really been asleep, due to an unexplained sharp click from the dashboard of the car that disturbed my brain every few minutes of the short and chilly night.

I thought it came from the clock but couldn't be sure. It was a coma rather than good slumber. Huge lorries roared along the motorway by which I was parked, going to Lille or Paris, and taking a few minutes to cross the battlefield of the Somme, some of whose acres were now buried under this broad, swathing highway.

Stirring myself, I took a gulp of brandy. It was half past three, with a faint light in the east, and I thought that a dawn attack at this time of the summer would have meant no rest at all, men dying in a half dream as they stumbled forward, or only waking to the pain of being wounded.

I drove along the empty road to Bapaume, and then southeast up to Flers and Longueval, where the outlines of hedges and fields were sharply enough etched for me to switch off the car lights. It was four o'clock, and no one was yet awake, all shutters being closed. Heavy mist lay in the hollows, but the land was wide open and rolling, high against the sky, with intensely dark patches of wood here and there. Faint scars showed where fighting took place, particularly on the edges of Delville Wood, in which thousands perished on both sides.

The same could be said of High Wood, and I drove to it slowly from Longueval, the sky leaden and the birds still noisy, but the half-kilometre flank of packed trees facing south was formidable up the gentle slope, stolid and uninviting even now in the dawn. The British, led for once by the cavalry, captured it on 14 July 1916, but, owing to the failure to take it several hours earlier than they did, when it was empty, and to get up reinforcements to hold it properly, they were thrown out. Waves of attacking infantry passed through it, or stayed in it, and it was not finally taken till after two months of the most dogged and costly fighting of the war.

I walked up the lane hoping to enter the wood, but it was fenced off and, as of old, one needed wire-cutters to get into it. Words on a board stated that trespassers would be prosecuted. Perhaps similar notices had been there in 1916 when the British unexpectedly broke through to it. Had the soldiers wondered, in any case, when they were launched in attack after attack, what had been the name of the man who owned the wood? Where was he at the time? Did he know that British soldiers were being mown down in hundreds because they were trying to get his wood back from the Germans?

Did he realise, wherever he was and whoever he was, that they were being bled and mangled for the sake of his half-kilometre square of tree-covered land? If he had seen them dying outside the wood, and burning to death inside, would he have wanted them to go on trying to get it back for him? What property was worth so much? Surely it would have been better to have gone up to the Germans under a flag of truce and made some attempt at paying them to get out.

And when those British battalions at last captured that bit of smoking, tree-ruined land, considering the price they had had to pay, who would it belong to then? It was the sort of awkward question my Uncle Frederick liked to put. Should it not have been theirs? It could surely be nobody else's after that big shindig. But they'd been brought up to respect other peoples' property, even to die for it in thousands, which was a somewhat unfathomable passion since none of them had any of their own. The most they'd say perhaps is that if anybody deserved High Wood it was the dead, but that was a trick, because since the dead were dead and had no way of speech, and in any case couldn't read notices saying that trespassers would be prosecuted, then it must go back to its private owner, waiting to claim its few charred trunks. One might declare that a notice such as faced me is better than a hail of bullets, but either way, one can't get in, which makes one wonder what it was all for.

Concerning this sacredness of property, it was a common though jocular belief among British soldiers during the Great

War that their government had to pay rent to the French for
the land the trenches were dug on.

A man who turns himself into a soldier becomes someone
else's property. But he should never do anything unless he first
asks himself: 'Why?' – and tries to square the action he is
about to take with his own conscience. To disobey orders is a
virtue, and if one is then alone after taking the responsibility
for it, one exists in a state of grace, and becomes a hero of
humanity.

49

I thought of walking in the field where my Uncle Edgar had
lain while waiting to be captured, but I didn't want to disturb
his shadow, which must still have been on it.

From the low stone wall of Gommecourt Wood Cemetery I
looked through binoculars at the space of that pathetic little
battlefield Edgar had walked across in such terror. It was not
holed and pitted now, of course, but was a rather wide, dipping
meadow of rich green grass that fifty years ago had fed on
blood.

The cemetery itself was placed by the laneside, on the
British frontline – or perhaps just a little into no-man's-land. I
don't know how many graves there were in this neat place – so
scrupulously kept. Many headstones had no names, or words
except: 'A Soldier of the Great War', or 'Known Only unto
God.'

At a later hour on Sunday morning I went into Aveluy
Wood, in the valley of the Ancre. The trees were grown up
again, but not to any great stature, though inside it was dark
enough to keep out the light. The still pitted ground had no
recognisable paths along the livid summer greenery, whereas
the pre-1914 maps showed many. Banks of earth were piled
above shallow yet distinct trenches. Bits of rusty wire and iron

spikes, pieces of shovel and decaying steel were scattered under leaves. If I dug I would have found bones, but I walked over ground that four battalions of West Yorkshiremen had taken cover in before making their futile attack against Thiepval on 1 July 1916.

Like other belligerent nations of the Great War the British have no defence against the charge of internal slaughter, of self-indulgent flag-waving, of a national, patriotic, suicidal lemming-rush, of the right hand smashing the left with such unfeeling brutality that both arms are still crippled more than half a century later. These are the unstated views of people I grew up among, of Frederick and his brother Edgar, the composite reactions to catastrophe of those whose words are not supposed to matter as far as history is concerned. But these myths have soaked themselves into the backbone of the country, and such unwritten emotional history will take generations to defuse.

The wood was defended by London battalions of the 47th Division when the British front swung away from the Germans at the beginning of April 1918, and there was savage hand-to-hand fighting with heavy loss of life on both sides. Undoubtedly there were many bones under the soil. Northern France is a vast bone-yard – British, German, and native French – and four million corpses rotted there. Why had they left their wives, children and parents to fight and die in this patch of wood? Were they so bored that they became belligerent and patriotic to cure it? Or was it true, as many said, that war was invented to keep massacre away from the homely fireside?

England, for so long the balcony from which one observed European revolutions, was dragged into an unnecessary revolution in 1914 by the scruff of its own neck, off with a wave and a smiling cheerio to help gallant little Belgium and threatened France. The upper classes were bored after late-Victorian stagnation and Edwardian good living, and wanted at the same time to cup the stirring body of the oppressed country. It seemed to fit in so well, everything coming together with such force that it almost makes one believe in God, in order to think that the Devil got into them.

Yet I come across the stray but galling reflection that if I had been alive at the time and twenty years of age I too might have allowed myself to be drummed into the slaughter – unless, being like my Uncle Frederick, I opted out with the closely-guarded integrity of my native sense. I am enough like him to have done that, though no one can finally say.

I picked up a marlin spike and for a moment considered taking it as a souvenir, but the idea seemed ludicrous so I threw it down. Huge quantities of scrap metal and live ammunition are collected every year from the wheal of the Western Front. Tons of unexploded artillery shells are encountered just under the soil, especially in woods, and people are often killed or maimed by them.

My feet were occasionally trapped in the undergrowth, legs buckling when some hidden trench or shellhole opened below. There were ghosts all around – though I laughed at the insane notion of it – and no noise except for the brush of my own passing, and the crack of dead, overfed twigs. I stood and listened, and couldn't get away from Edward Elgar's music which kept coming into my mind. I disliked it at such a time, but there was nothing to be done about it. Let the ghosts haunt the ghosts, and spiders weave their webs. It was bad to be alone in such a place.

But the time of the world was up, when the blood-letting came among these trees. Apart from the matter of revolution, the emotional sensuousness that was matched to a hundred years of romanticism and repression burst into a slaughter-house. The music of Sibelius and Mahler led straight into the trenches. They didn't see it then, but we can see it now. Truth (for what it was worth) hauled the uniformed masses over the top by the scruff of the neck and the grip of the genitals. We haven't finished here yet, nor in any way understood it.

What happened indeed to the peace one was supposed to find in the middle of a wood? I walked in the direction I had come, hoping it would take me to the car, though by keeping a straight line I would obviously reach some lane or other, and escape from this verdant spirit-haunt.

But it is impossible to escape from Elgar – whether or not one is in Aveluy Wood. He is a real artist, a man of complete conscience, England's greatest composer certainly, for he not only sent the men into the trenches but greeted them when

126

they came out. He beat in the other ranks with Pomp and Circumstance Marches, and nodded the commissioned officers in to the Introduction and Allegro for Strings. When they returned he met these broken men with the infinite sadness and pity of the Violincello Concerto in E minor. This work contains the broken bones of Edwardian glory and an attempt at semi-jovial rebirth, never taken seriously, as if he could not get over the fact that his most enduring work was to be built on a million corpses.

He wants to be gay in the second movement, but the Angel of Mons is too much in the ascendant. There is a crater under his heels which he edges warily away from. In the third section his tetric phrases meander through the ranks of his million ghosts. In his bucolic English way he expresses sorrow and regret that the world had gone the way it did – even though he may have been in some small sense responsible.

But finally the energy overcomes him and he says: 'I am an artist and so can't be to blame. If I set your subconscious to music, much as I might with any poet's words, then I am only being myself as an artist.'

The vibrant yet wistful strength of the body slowly rises. As a composer his best works show him to be a man of the people, but out of the whole people. As an artist he tried to unify – that was his purpose – as any artist's must be. That was his wish, and I suppose at various times of his life, particularly before 1914, he thought that he might even be succeeding. But like any artist, part of him was blind, and it wasn't till 1918 that he saw how wrong he had been, and that some disaster had occurred which had smashed his beloved England for a long time to come. So his concerto is a work of sadness, regret and hope. The broken body of England was dragging itself back through the mud of Passchendaele. It still haunts the resurrected woods of the Somme.

History, meantime, goes on. We love Mahler, we crave to hear Sibelius. They are artists, after all. And bourgeois capitalism is cured of its worst rampages of war because the Bomb, an effective weapon of peace, threatens not only people with total destruction, but *all property*, and no nation can bring itself to risk such a price. Property is God, and this age-old

127

enemy of the people turns out at last to be its final safeguard, behind which we can go on enjoying the works of our favourite artists and try to live.

Walking through the cemetery of Gommecourt and the vast collection of graveyards around Ypres, where tens of thousands rest under crosses or the occasional Star of David, the feeling is one of bewilderment and pity that brings tears like a wall of salt up to the eyes. When there are too many people in the world the dead take up less space than the living. Even those who hate war have their idea of a just war, a war that people in the future will no doubt pronounce to have been as stupid as the rest.

I was lost, and began to wonder if I would ever get out. No longer amused at my lack of orientation, I stopped and lit a cigarette. There had been too many murders here in Aveluy Wood, too many state-sanctioned church-blessed killings, too much confused death, too many mistakes – society's mincing-machine for its unwanted energy and talent.

Yet I knew there could be many surprises in the journey after death, especially for a soldier. The killing in the Great War was on so massive a scale that a decent number of corpses could be collected into cemeteries and put under the soil, a final resting place as far as we know. Many dead of the Napoleonic Wars, however, went through a different fate, as I was reminded on reading the following paragraph from *The Observer* of 18 November 1822:

'It is estimated that more than a million bushels of human and inhuman bones were imported last year from the continent of Europe into the port of Hull. The neighbourhood of Leipsig, Austerlitz, Waterloo and of all the places where, during the late bloody war, the principal battles were fought, have been swept alike of the bones of the hero and the horse which he rode. Thus collected from every quarter, they have been shipped from the port of Hull and thence forwarded to the Yorkshire bone grinders who have erected steam-engines and powerful machinery for the purpose of reducing them to a granulary state. In this condition they are sold to the farmers to manure their lands.'

50

The oldest man killed in the Great War was 68; the youngest a boy of 15 from Southend who had joined up from school before his 14th birthday. A father who lost his 20-year-old son was so stricken that he too, at over forty, joined up to get his revenge and was also killed. A recent notice appeared in the 'In Memoriam' column of *The Times*:

'Robinson. – In treasured memory of 2nd Lt. Peter Robinson, 7th Battalion North Loamshire Regiment, killed in action, May 1940; and of his adored father Captain Peter Robinson, Border Regiment, killed in action 1917 – Mother.'

Telegrams were worded in the following manner: 'I regret to inform, War Office reports Lieut. K. H. Moore 4th North Lancashire Regt. was killed November 26th. Lord Kitchener expresses his sympathy.'

A few days later (December 4th) came the additional: 'The King and Queen deeply regret the loss you and the Army have sustained by the death of your Son in the service of his country. Their Majesties truly sympathise with you in your sorrow.'

Soldiers died in many ways; the wastage of life behind the Front was also heavy as extracts from letters show: 'Your husband (aged 30) met his end through heart failure brought on by suffocation. With six pals he went to sleep in a van. They had the windows and doors shut and . . . your husband was found dead and the others unconscious. He was the best driver in the section.'

'Driver Porter (aged 18) was the centre driver of a wagon which was laying cable near Martinsart. Porter was tightening up the harness when two shells fell fairly close. The horses bolted, the rear part of the wagon passing over his legs. He was an excellent soldier. He died of his injuries.'

'Aged 38 – accidentally killed whilst getting on to a motor lorry; his foot slipped and a wheel passed over him. His cheery smile will be missed by us all very much.' – A comrade.

Lance-Corporal Johnstone – 'released from Army December 1918 – died of tuberculosis from the effects of captivity in Germany, at Southend, September 27th, 1920, aged 26.'

'Corporal Jordan died of gunshot wounds, at Douai, April 1st, 1918, whilst a prisoner in German hands.'

'Private Treby, Machine Gun Corps, aged 27. Serving with the orchestra attached to 33rd Infantry Brigade, was killed by a shell whilst playing on the piano with the orchestra a selection of his own composition. The brigade orchestra, in which he was the most important artiste, was well known throughout France, and had done a great deal to brighten up the men and make their lives happier.'

Thus wrote the officer commanding his battalion to his mother. Thus the catalogue of death goes on.

My foot touched solid ground. I was alive, so through the treetops of Aveluy Wood took a healthy line on the sun – still easterly in the sky – and walked till I came to a lane. Using a map, I soon reached the open, glad to be away from trees that had smelled so many corpses they seemed almost human.

51

A photograph of my Uncle Frederick, which was taken before 1914 and blended neatly with the older man I came to know, shows an acute and ironic expression, a face both forceful and sensitive, with thin, down-curving lips which could not have boded too well for anyone who became emotionally involved with him, nor indeed for the man who actually wore such a face.

An intelligent man, he also had that pride and assurance which led him to believe that his self-education had fitted him at least as much for civilised life as those who had been formally instructed and indoctrinated.

He was about thirty when the Great War began, a small

man like his father, with dark hair and brown eyes, the eldest and most cultured son of the family. He was gifted in his trade of lace-designer, a job which combined the sort of art and technical skill that his temperament had been made for. He travelled in it a good deal before 1914. Finding it difficult to sell his patterns in Nottingham, or being dissatisfied with the prices offered, he went to London, and bought a second-class return ticket for £5 11s 8d to the German textile town of Chemnitz, hoping for better luck.

He stayed in London long enough to go to a concert at the Albert Hall, which began with Wagner's Overture to *Tannhaüser*. This, he said, was one of the most thrilling experiences of his life. From then on he was a split enough personality, due to the two differing layers of music which ran concurrently almost through the whole piece, to deal with the modern world – as he saw it then – for such was the new psychic equipment just revealed to him. The mind had many layers, not just one, and if you were fazed in one part, if one section was vanquished, the other immediately came into play with its untouched energy and fresh intelligence.

Yet apart from this view, which he saw as somewhat mechanical if too closely examined, the music inspired him with the belief that the world was a rich and wonderful place. He had a trade in which he felt himself to be talented, he was on his travels and in his mid-twenties, and the open world before him seemed an eternally eventful expanse that would stay that way for ever, with the occasional feasts of such wonderful music to bathe his heart and soul and so remind him of it.

'I had no idea,' he said, 'that it was too good to last.'

The 700-mile journey to Chemnitz took thirty-five hours, and on arrival he set to work making appointments. One firm was impressed by his designs, and the manager took him to a meal at the opulent Stadt Gotha Hotel while they were being examined by the directors. But when they returned to the office the manager gave the designs back, regretting that his factory would be unable to use them, though hoping that he would come back one day and let them see more.

This was a big dip from their first enthusiasm. He politely accepted his portfolio, but then said to the directors who had

131

come to wish him goodbye: 'Would you now give me back the copies you made of my drawings while I was out enjoying your kind hospitality at the hotel?'

'The atmosphere was so tense,' he said, 'that you could have chopped it with a battle-axe. But I was on to their bloody schemes – because it had happened to me once before in England.'

Frederick repeated his sentence in even blunter language, and their anger at his accusation gave way to embarrassment, then to humour when they realised he had seen through their trick. But it was *their* humour, and not his, so they bought his patterns, and paid him generously.

He went again to sell his designs. The manager, Herr Schmidt, invited him to a meal in his pretty Saxon villa on the outskirts of the town – a substantial house walled by trees and lined with flowers on that close and thundery summer's day. They were driven up the cobbled street from the factory in Herr Schmidt's large open motor car. Workpeople bowed to them from the pavements. Frederick wondered what in God's name he was doing there.

But he made enough money to visit nearby Dresden, that Florence-on-the-Elbe with its famous galleries, palaces and collections, the first great 'artistic' city he had seen outside London. The most beautiful women of Europe lived in Dresden: a subtle, cosmopolitan meeting point of all creeds and races. The Saxon princes were among the richest sovereigns in Europe, for their nearby silver mines had been an immense source of wealth before the discovery of America. Art flourished for centuries, and vast treasures were accumulated for the delectation of the whole continent.

Frederick revelled in it, a young man out from Nottingham with money in his pocket and a secondhand Baedeker guidebook in his pack – who saw himself so much the equal of any man that he didn't even have to think about it. He recalled the city forty years later when his thin, ageing face took on colour against the British for destroying it at the end of the Second World War. He saw it as an act of catastrophic spite, a killing of two birds with one stone in which the mass of the people

were wiped out at the same time as the architectural treasures
of the old aristocracy.

'The Nazi swine looted,' he said, 'and the British burned.
The British hatred for Europe has always been the lynchpin of
their wars and diplomacy. They talk about a balance of power,
but all they want to do is sink it. Why else did they destroy
beautiful Dresden?'

'It was part of the R.A.F. policy,' I said, 'to dehouse the
German workers.'

'If they did that then to the *German* workers,' he responded,
'I wonder what they'd do to our own if ever they got uppity?'

52

Chemnitz has altered considerably since Frederick was there,
sixty years ago. The centre was obliterated by the R.A.F.
Nowadays it is the great textile city of the German Demo-
cratic Republic, and is known as Karlmarxstadt.

I went there, and visited a textile plant – in the footsteps, it
seemed, of my uncle. In the middle of the central square of
this pleasant Saxon city, surrounded by elegant blocks of flats
and shops, is a huge head of Karl Marx himself, a massive and
solid juff hewn in reddish stone, and set without neck or
shoulders on a plinth.

The last time Frederick saw the place was at the end of July
1914. He left his hotel, which in the morning smelled strongly
of boot polish and coffee, and took a tram to the station. A
nearby shop provided him with bread and sausage for the
journey. He stood on the platform waiting for the train to
Berlin, and reading *David Copperfield* in the early morning
light, avid to get on with the novel because he was up to the
point where David, as a young man who had just finished his
education in Canterbury, was going away with a pocketful of
money for a month's travelling.

From this time till the North Sea we don't know in the family what happened, because Frederick never filled in the gap either for them or for me, except to say that on the way from Berlin he witnessed the mobilisation manoeuvres of the Imperial German Army near Magdeburg. Whether this was intentional or not I have no idea, but he made a dramatic farewell to the country because the police tried to arrest him at Bremerhaven for what he had seen.

For generations, he recalled, the name of Germany had meant 'culture'. It was, as everyone said, the most 'cultured' country in Europe. But, Frederick went on, that did not by any means make it the most human. Science and energy it had, artists, writers and composers it had, but you saw, if you travelled with a soul in your body, that there was much else besides which was not always buried very far beneath the surface.

The swooning experience of his first Wagner concert did not last long. Culture had never been synonymous with humanity and peaceful intentions – either in England or in Germany. But with the most powerful army in the world, and a modern navy rapidly building, the Kaiser and many of his people were quickly becoming the bully of the world. A man can hear Beethoven's Ninth Symphony with tears in his eyes, then go outside and club someone with his rifle butt. Culture, even as far down as your toenails, need make no damned difference at all. You must also love humanity, not only in general but also very much in particular. A country can be highly cultured – as undoubtedly most of them were in 1914 – but unless its inhabitants are respecters of humanity, watch out. In fact it might be that the more cultured a country is the more dangerous it becomes, especially if that reputation for culture has adhered for so long that it is harnessed to pride and nationalism, and works in such a way that it stifles conscience.

Frederick's ship pulled out from the quay just as the police came into view. Or, at any rate, it was something as close as that. He left for England only hours before war was declared. If they had collared him he would have spent four years in the Ruhleben internment camp for civilians near Berlin, and thus saved himself some bother in trying to avoid the war in his own country.

The sea-crossing was so appallingly rough that he was unable to leave his cabin.

53

When call-up came in 1916 Frederick would have nothing to do with it, averring that a person who refused to get killed for his country is more patriotic than a mad keen bravo who rushes into death for it, that a man is of more value to everyone else if he stays alive. He was not alone in his reluctance to go, for in the first six months of conscription 100,000 men failed to appear for call-up, and another 750,000 hurried to claim exemption.

His wife belonged to the Christadelphians and Frederick had been converted to this faith. Whether before or after marriage I could not say, but 'Christadelphians,' he told me, 'is Greek for "Brothers of Christ".' They are also known – or were, he went on – as Thomasites, being a religious group founded in 1848 (of all years!) by one John Thomas (1805–1871) in the United States. He was born in England and, after studying medicine in London, emigrated to Brooklyn.

The name 'Christadelphians' was taken during the American Civil War, when they had to justify a total objection to military service. There is no distinction between clergy and laity among them. Their faith is based on the Hebrew Prophecy and the Book of Revelation. Its members meet on Sunday to 'break bread' and discuss the Bible.

Frederick likened the Christadelphians to those small Bible-loving Protestant communities of Reformation days, whose aim was to get as close to the First Century Church as possible. A founding tenet of their belief has always been that the Jewish people would return to, and recolonise, their land of Israel.

135

John Thomas himself wrote a book called *Elpis Israel* (Hope of Israel) stating this prophecy, which Frederick frequently mentioned.

John Thomas, the founding Christadelphian, informed his readers and followers that, before the Second Coming can take place, the Jewish people must be re-established in *Eretz Israel*. A recent pamphlet exults in the fact that this has been realised in the founding of Modern Israel, which points to the distinct possibility that the second major prophecy may soon come to pass. The Rock of Israel is refounded, and shall never be moved.

Frederick assiduously studied the Bible, and learned Hebrew in order to justify his membership, and it was his allegiance to this sect that led him to stand as a conscientious objector – an educated phrase unintelligible to most ordinary people, and which would have been better understood by them as just a plain 'non-believer in war'.

Facing the tribunal of old, true-blue British dunderheads who looked upon him with a sort of patriarchal distaste and offended class unction because he was staunchly refusing the honour of being sent to fight for what they held dear, and would no doubt lavishly enjoy after many of those who had gone to do so were dead, he simply stated his religious principles and folded his arms against them with such mute and obstinate belligerence that it caused one mellower gentleman to regret that such unyielding brass could not be turned against the Germans.

Having long ago weighed up his own talent as a lace-designer and painter of pictures, Frederick quoted his profession before these men as that of artist, upon which the mellower gentleman brightly wondered why he had not joined the Artists' Rifles when the war began, whose fine battalions did wonderfully dreadful work against the Hun.

Frederick broke his silence, though he had gritted his teeth for some ten minutes against doing so. 'There wasn't one artist in the Artists' Rifles,' he said sharply, and so angrily that he had to fight against his own blood to keep to the point of what he wanted to say. 'They stopped being artists as soon as they put on a uniform. No true artist picks up a gun to kill his fellow-men. Whoever had the idea to form battalions of artists was a devil. He was anti-Christ. It was Satan's trick, to get rid of those artists who might otherwise stay behind and make trouble – or keep a breath of sanity in this country. If any artists are still fighting they are poor deluded fools who don't deserve their talent. In all likelihood they never had any.'

The two sides were without meeting point, and instead of being sent into the army Frederick spent two years shovelling shit – as he put it – on a farm in Lincolnshire.

'Man chooses,' he said, 'though God disputes his right to it. Freedom of choice is given to everyone, and if I lived in the moderate comfort of a hayloft instead of cringing in a mud-trench in Flanders, then I betrayed no one, because everybody else could have done the same. They made the wrong choice, and it led to the biggest disaster in the history of the world, because the Second World War came out of the First, and the Jews were almost destroyed by Hitler and his lunatic pan-Germans, and by all those others who didn't say a big enough No when they should have done. The only things you can say yes to in this world are love and work, and even then you've got to be intelligent and careful about it. God knows, I'm not made of such stuff that my life's been all that successful, but I've never killed or injured anybody.'

During his agricultural life he and his companions were awakened from the hayloft opposite the house at five each morning to the tune of a bully-farmer cracking a whip below, and cursing so richly that it might have sounded picturesque if it hadn't been aimed at them. To the farmer they were work-horses, and weak ones who did not have the necessary patriotic feeling to go and fight for their country so that he could stay behind and make a profit from it. They were scum, worse even than prisoners of war, who might at least have fair reason for being out of the fighting.

Nocturnally roaming around and into remote sheds of the farm, Frederick and a friend discovered a small trunk hidden under a heap of sacks. On shaking it, they rightly guessed that it contained several hundred gold sovereigns. As the Great War went on the government needed gold to pay its debts, so a law was passed that such coinage was to be handed in to the banks, who would then issue the equivalent in paper money. It was illegal to hoard such metal, though many did – so as to sell it after the war when its value would be much increased.

Next day the conscientious objectors carried the box to the farmer's door. When he came at the jingle of it, Frederick said in his most pompous and grating tone that they expected his behaviour to improve from now on, as a reward for finding his long-lost gold. But if the farmer was not the real owner of it, then it should be taken to the police station in Louth. If he was, which seemed likely because they had found it on his property, then it should be put into a bank for safe keeping.

The farmer disliked them, but accepted his gold and treated them more reasonably afterwards. He never found out who had broken the lock of the shed where the box had been kept, though he had his suspicions. As Frederick said, delicate fingers can always be put to good use.

54

We lived in a room on Talbot Street whose four walls smelled of leaking gas, stale fat, and layers of mouldering wallpaper. My father's thirty-year-old face was set like concrete, ready to hold back the tears of humiliation that he must have been pleased to find were not there when the plain-clothes police came to take him away.

From the side I saw two of him as he combed his black hair in the mirror. The face looking into the glass seemed about to smile, but that reflected from it showed the bafflement of his brown eyes, and lips that were thinner when he was unhappy. In both images his flesh was grey.

He had especially gloated over his brother Frederick's haughty manner with creditors. Being dunned as a young man during one of his indigent phases after his release from the servitude of the Great War, Frederick stood at the door of his father's shop on Trafalgar Street with, as my father remembered: 'Hardly any bleddy shoes to his feet', shouting at a tradesman waiting hopefully on the pavement: 'I only pay my bills quarterly! Do you understand? Quarterly!'

That night a pantechnicon was loaded to the gills by my father and the driver, Frederick looking on because his hands were too fine to lift such heavy goods and furniture on which little more than a deposit had been paid. The pantechnicon went to London where, as far as the creditors were concerned, Frederick was never heard of again, London being a long way from Nottingham in those days.

Years later, when my father was married, unemployed, and already had three kids to feed, he tried the same scheming stunt of running up bills for food that he had no hope of paying, an imitation of his elder brother which turned out to be the highest form of folly, for he lacked Frederick's superior mobility and ways of speech when the shopkeeper asked him to pay up or get taken to court. But even when he came back from prison he was glad his brother had been able to beat the system from time to time, and often gloated over it to me.

Frederick followed his trade of lace and embroidery designer in London, and for a while he was a court embroiderer, though I omitted to ask what court because I suspected he was exaggerating his claim to grandeur – which might have been doing him an injustice. But there was a great slump in his trade by the middle thirties, and he was thrown as much out of work as were Burton and his sons when motor-cars finished off blacksmithery.

In 1936 he met a column of unemployed miners that had stopped to rest at some open ground before continuing their march to the middle of London. Various members of it went among the spectators with collecting boxes, gathering funds to buy food and shoes for the men. A great many police stood at various points of the concourse, not expecting purple revolution to break out there and then so much as to intimidate them into knowing their place by the time they reached the middle of London – where hosepipes were waiting for them anyway. Frederick, moved by the men's plight, put the large sum of half a crown into a box, at which a police inspector told him brusequely to get out of the way and move on.

139

In a tone of congenital intransigence Frederick retorted that it was his right to give to whom he pleased. The policeman left him alone, and went after the man with the collecting box. Telling me about it fifteen years later, the incident still infuriated him more, I think, because a man in uniform had dared to accost him on any pretext whatsoever, than that the hunger-marchers had been harried.

He was widely read, and the most politically radical of the family, though his radicalism was of a somewhat uncertain brand – when he allowed it to show through. Perhaps his intensive reading of the Old Testament made him so, and his experiences as a conscientious objector left him as bitter against government, British or otherwise, of past, present and future, as any soldier who by a miracle had survived four years in the trenches.

Parting from his wife and two daughters, he came back to Nottingham in 1936. He also broke with the Christadelphian sect (after more than twenty years of it) and turned atheist. Or so he said, but he kept his fine theological library, and was never without a pile of books from it on his table. I certainly never heard him say a word against the sect to which he had once belonged; and during many extempore sermons in my presence he often invoked God's name and extolled the virtues ('as well as the necessity, in this savage world') of religion.

When I first met him in 1949 I had started to think of myself as a writer. 'A good short story,' he advised me, 'is what people want. It's what editors are looking for, as well.' To back up his point he sent me to Nottingham Central Library with lists of books to take out and read.

He was sixty-five years old, and worked at his studio desk with a skullcap on the back of his bald head. Having a thin, wax-like face, his features resembled those of Voltaire's death-mask (a plaster copy of which hung from the wall above his desk as a measure of his admiration for that great man) if one caught him asleep or having just woken up.

Though quite prosperous for certain periods of his life, Frederick had dressed well but never really ate properly, as if that side of good comfort didn't interest him. So he kept a frail unhealthy aspect, though he fetched more than eighty years of age.

He lived, in his second Nottingham period, in two small rooms, high up in an old building of Nottingham's Lacemarket district, whose factories he had so hopefully and for a time successfully traipsed thirty years before to sell his designs. In 1940–41 when bombs fell all around he never went down to the air raid shelters.

The rooms were rented as a 'studio', and it was unlawful to live in them, but the police and people who knew turned a blind eye to it, and in any case, didn't an artist work through the night, as well as by day?

The two years I knew him I listened for hours to his monologues on literature, religion and politics, and to his preaching. It seemed strange that the first educated person I met should belong, after all, to my own family.

'The most bitter fact,' he said, 'that you have to live with, is that you can't bring back history. You can't remake the past. You can't remodel it in any tiny way. You can't alter the present, either, even though you know that one day *that* also will be "history" – from the viewpoint of the future. If ever one is able to properly see the present from the vantage point of the future perhaps it will be feasible to do something about making the present a little less terrible.

'Man isn't wise enough to see things that way. For where, asks Job, shall wisdom be found? Where is the place of understanding? "Man knoweth not the price thereof;" ' – he quoted – ' "neither is it found in the land of the living." But that wonderful heartrending 28th chapter of Job ends by saying: "the fear of the Lord, that is wisdom; and to depart from evil is understanding."

'You can't get away from it: such basic morality admits neither of misinterpretation, nor backsliding. God may be indifferent to suffering, but we must believe in his goodness all the same. The afflicted have to trust in God; the happy have to fear him. "Did not he that made me in the womb make him?" Job cried out. He realised the great truth that he and God were made of and by the same thing. He knew though that men must fear God and that "he respecteth not any that are wise of heart." Try and beat that sort of language if you can!'

He talked for hours on painting and art. His drawings were fine and meticulous. Now and again I would sit for him, and much of his work must still be scattered around Nottingham, for the only way he earned money at that time was by selling landscapes and doing portraits. Needing little at this part of his life made him a man of independent means, in the sense that those who have little, but which is all they need, can afford the most freedom.

An obsessional expatriator, he wanted a listener, and there was none better than an incipient writer for whom he could dip into his reminiscences and tap endless pipelines of information. He told me about a spiritual exercise by which he viewed any troublesome problem in its own utter light, and therefore went much of the way to solving. He concentrated his mind until there was nothing left in it, then went on to force his nothingness to an even greater pitch of vacuity, so that in the blinding light of emptiness the problem suddenly reappeared with such clarity that the answer was obvious. Think of nothing, was how he put it, and think on that.

He loved England, but did not like it, and would lunge at the good name of its indwellers as often as some sharp light flashing from past or present forced him to:

'The English are a nation of form-fillers,' he would say, putting a few flourishes to the cloud of a half-finished land-scape. I remembered this picture as a remote, mellow, dream-like hilly country without people or even animals, some peaceful therapeutic land he could escape into after spending too much time on the close-up detail of his portraits.

'In some countries,' he went on, pausing a moment to get into his best hectoring rhythm, 'when the backbone has cracked, they live by taking in each other's washing. In dear old England they exchange forms to fill in. Give somebody a form and he won't tear it up and throw the bits back at you. Not your Englishman, he won't. He'll get out his pen and wonder how to fill it in so as to please and satisfy whoever made it up. They'll let authority put chains on them as long as it respects their privacy. They don't want to be touched, ergo – ergot – (or is it argot?) – they'll sign anything.'

'Well,' I said, not really objecting to his statement, nor his punning, 'you're English. And so am I. You can't get away from it.'

'True,' he admitted. 'At least I expect it is. I was born on the island, and that's a fact. *You* still have time to get off it, if you look sharp in the way of saving yourself. In any case, I'm an artist. I'm independent. But think about it: the war's been over six years, and the English still put up with rationing and conscription. Anybody who tries to get a tiddly bit of food above his fair share is denounced as a traitor and a black-marketeer, whereas it's only a healthy and normal reaction to an unnecessary restriction. And don't think they won't always be like this, even when such vicious things are finished with. Scratch an Englishman and you find a – no, not only a Turk – but a ration book, or an identity card, or a pay-book, or a census form or even a form from the back of the *Radio Times* to order a greenhouse or potting shed. In other words, a form to fill in lets them know their place, and they love that.'

'Every country is the same,' I said, to see whether or not he had finished. 'It's called modern civilisation, in case you didn't know.'

'Civilisation, my arse!' he cried, throwing his brush aside and reaching out to fill the kettle – or shutting off his monologue with acerbity when he wanted to clear his room and get down to work: 'It's killed too many innocent people in the last fifty years for any intelligent man to think there's much good in it.'

Those were his final words – on that occasion. He certainly didn't seem like my father's brother, yet there was little doubt that he was.

55

A nest of brothers is a dangerous thing, whether or not they are different, especially to the man who spermed them out. Bert was the second eldest and, at seventeen, during a savage quarrel with his father, picked up a hobbing-iron from the floor of the upholstery shop and threw it with all his might towards the head he could no longer stand the sight of.

He missed – a failure he regretted for the rest of his life. Ashamed of the regret, whose twinges came sharply on him as soon as he saw his father's whitened face still intact, he rushed out of the house swearing never to come back.

After a few days on the streets there seemed nothing else to do but go for a soldier, which he did with the South Notts Hussars, who were being fitted up for service in the Boer War. When his mother got wind of his enlistment she wrote to the Army Office to say he was too young for active service, and had him called off the troopship at Southampton an hour before it left.

It was as well he didn't go, for the regiment supposedly disgraced itself in South Africa by refusing to charge at well-hidden and deadly Boer rifles, many troopers having already been killed and wounded because of the slovenly tactical arrangements of their officers. It was due to these casualties that Lord Roberts, one of the commanders in the war, was booed and hissed when he led a parade into Nottingham at the end of it.

Bert went home to an uneasy parental truce and got work with a firm of upholsterers. He enlisted as a cavalryman when the Great War began, and was on guard at a camp outside Boulogne when the horses broke loose one night during an air-raid. One of them kicked so violently that his arm was broken in three places, and he was stunned by agony, unable to get off the ground. An officer who saw him lying there shouted that he was trying to hide from the bombs, adding that if he didn't stand up like a man and go about his business he would have him court-martialled.

Bert's response was not clear enough to be heard through the noise of gunfire and bombs, and the officer thought he was being insolent instead of explanatory, so lifted his stick with the intention of hitting him if he didn't get back to work. Night, uneasy horses, loud bangs of anti-aircraft guns, and the sweat of fast-running panic created a permanent nightmare. To Bert war seemed to have spread over everything human and animal, even back to the dreamy recesses of his past life – which now seemed idyllic. It was as if it had gone for ever in the great rattle-bang of the midnight sky, and he blamed the young but bloodshot face fixed near by.

Rage overcame his pain and shot him to his feet, and he threatened to smash the officer with his one good fist if he didn't get out of the way. He was surprised at the effect of his action, but glad nevertheless, for the officer sidestepped him and walked quickly to another part of the camp in case his historical ability to restore order should be impaired at the present place before it had had time to go into action there. Bert never forgave him for thinking he was a coward, and for treating him, he said, as German officers were said to treat their own men.

In the darker moments of his subsequent life he was haunted by the encounter, which he worked into a well-endowed focus for his personal hatred. The officer fully intended to have him court-martialled for insubordination but desisted when told of the smashed arm, though he did not apologise or make any comment. Such was the way in which the 'splendid material of the New Armies' was treated. For the first time men of self-respect were brought up against the brutal realities of what they had committed themselves to defend.

Perhaps the Great War conveniently used up Bert's excess of spirit, for when it finished he was content to work at his craft as upholsterer. He did not want to take over his father's business, though only he had the skill and perseverance to do so, but stayed the rest of his life at one firm. He was an elderly man when I knew him, a quiet person who had the reputation of keeping very much to himself. By then he was proud of the fact that he had been employed for so long at the same place, one of whose workshops had his own name over the door.

Yet he had more inner turmoil to contend with than his brothers, a restlessness that curbed any ambition, so that he needed all his energy to live a normal life. It was hard to imagine, seeing that bald, glint-eyed man sitting by the fire with a pipe between his teeth which he wouldn't always take out to talk in his clear and measured voice, that he'd joined the cavalry during two wars, and had been a daredevil in horsemanship.

His brothers testified to his prowess as a rider, saying that his absolute way with horses was due to human strength, animal sympathy, and a cunning that blended both. Frederick said he'd taken well to the military life from time to time, even describing him as something of a martinet, which may have been because he was the only one of the six sons to rebel against his father.

But there was something of the tethered horse in him too, of a man who knew how to tame a horse and who realised that he also had been broken in, and placed firmly under the domestic saddle. Perhaps life would have been insupportable if he hadn't, yet in an unguarded moment he allowed one to see his unsettled eyes wondering what he was doing in the imprisoning parlour where he sat and told his tale. He was the only one of my father's family who was connected in spirit to the Burtons, though as far as I know he never met any of them.

56

Edgar snubbed the roses of Picardy by surviving the Great War as a prisoner of the Germans, then went back to work for his father. He married some time during the twenties, but his wife left him after a few months. She accused him of leading her an unspeakable life, while he in his brooding silence could not begin to fathom what she meant.

My sister talked about life at the Sillitoes when I saw her in Nottingham City Hospital just before she died of cancer. She remembered further back than ever before, and recalled a visit to their shop when she was four or five. I must have been with her as well but, being barely two years of age, had no memory of it.

We spent much of the time playing on the stairs while sharp

arguments went on in one of the rooms. The ground floor of the house consisted of the shop and work-alcoves. On the next floor was a large lounge and the living quarters, and the top storey was occupied by several bedrooms.

Perhaps they were talking about who should take over the business when the old man died, an honour which eventually fell to my father. It meant little that he could not read or write, because in those days there were many such men who nevertheless prospered. And he had been reasonably trained as an upholsterer, perhaps to make up for the early neglect.

However Edgar wanted it for himself, and talked him out of it with little difficulty, since my father was particularly soft-hearted where family affairs were concerned.

But Edgar lost control of the flourishing business in less than half a year because of his drinking. The shop – as my sister put it – had to be sold under him, and he then took up odd-jobbing and journeying in the upholstery trade. This might have given him a fair living, but he needed the oblivion or good-feeling of being drunk, and boozed all that he earned.

In our part of the family he was known as 'Eddie the Tramp', and now and again would come and bed down with us a few nights. As we were often destitute he must really have been at the end of his tether, though maybe it was the company of a brother and a few children he wanted, rather than the cups of tea and pieces of bread he'd get by way of food.

On each occasion he probably hoped to stay longer than he did, but my parents never managed his company for more than one night, suddenly deciding he drank too much, or stank too much, or said too little, or took up too much space in the small room, or stared at them when in fact he was only looking emptily at the wall. And then there'd be shouting, and he'd snatch at his cap and bag of tools, and be out of the door before either my sister or I knew what was going on.

He once spent Christmas with us when he hadn't slept in a bed for months, and smelled like it. My father gave him his spare shirt, and my mother sent him to the public baths before they closed, telling him not to call in any pub on the way back or there'd be no hot dinner for him.

We children were excited that Uncle Eddie was going to

stay at such a time, because nobody had done that before. In spite of his greasy raincoat, and cap the colour of ancient nicotine, and the fact that he'd come to us like a broken-down tramp, he had money on him, and the sum he mentioned so far exceeded the amount of my father's dole that we hoped he'd bring us comics and toffees on his way back from the baths. Being a gentle and quiet-spoken person who looked at us with respect, almost as if he were afraid of us, there was a chance he wouldn't forget. We also admired him because he'd got a trade, though at the same time it didn't seem much good to him.

He returned with two quart bottles of beer, plus sweets and comics, and a piece of meat wrapped in newspaper. His dark hair was neatly combed under his cap, and he'd had a shave at the barber's, a sprucing up which turned him back into a passably handsome youngish man of forty.

That night he slept on the sofa, and a bit of fire glowed in the grate for him. The next day there was cheerful talk of staying for good and paying a small amount for his board and lodging. He would have regular meals and be provided with a clean shirt every week, while the money he contributed would help us.

In the afternoon my sister and I sat at the table with pencil and paper, and Eddie amused us by drawing pictures of German soldiers, complete with the traditional helmets and rifle. A frosty wind was blowing up the valley of the Leen, but the house was warm and for us four children it was a good place to be.

But on Boxing Day some inexplicable quarrel erupted between the two brothers, and my father threw him out. Both my parents were glad to be rid of him, as if he'd been with us six months, though my sister and I were in tears because we knew he had nowhere to go in the bitter cold.

So he lived alone, and never washed or changed, in order perhaps that the sharp and pungent smell would give him a clearer sense of his own identity, and at the same time protect him from those who did not heed him. During the Second World War, when money was easier to come by and he took his earnings into the noisy pubs – the Albany, the Eight Bells, or the Trip to Jerusalem built snug against the sandstone sides of the Castle – he was a somewhat lugubrious free-spender, treating and tipping as if he thought it unlucky to get change from notes or silver, though nobody could seem as down on his luck when it was all gone and he was walking around the pubs and cinemas for more seating to mend or recondition.

His reputation for skill was well known on the circuit he had built up, and he could have jobs for the asking, though those who employed him were careful not to hand out any payment before he had finished. On moneyless nights he would occasionally receive a pint at the bar from some generous American soldier, who clearly saw a free-born Englishman down on his luck – odd gifts which Edgar gratefully accepted, for he too would treat soldiers of all nationalities when he had money.

I often earned good cash on piece-work, so when we met I'd give him a few bob if he was broke, which I usually knew him to be by the depressed look of his lips. Sometimes I was mistaken, and if he had money he would take nothing, and even with delicate frankness ask if I needed anything.

I last saw him on the top deck of a bus going from Radford into the middle of Nottingham. When we got off at Chapel Bar I gave him a copy of my first book of poems, called *Without Beer or Bread*, and he smiled at the title as he put it into his mackintosh pocket. I was about to go when, from an inside waistcoat, he brought an old fob-timepiece which he wanted me to have in exchange for the poems.

'I can't take your watch.'

He smiled, the few teeth left in his mouth gone rotten. 'It's only gold-plated zinc. It was with me at Gommecourt, and in Germany. Went all the time I was under fire. Would you believe it? Hasn't gone for years now.'

I looked at its clean Roman numerals on a round white face, a plain style I'd always liked, its two hands stopped at four o'clock. 'I often meant to get it going,' he said, 'but the pawnshop was closer than the watchmaker! They'd let me have a few bob on it but I'd allus redeem it before the time ran out.'

'Let me give you something for it,' I offered, knowing this wouldn't insult him if he was broke, and that he'd be offended if I didn't take the watch. He tapped his pocket with my book in it: 'Exchange is no robbery. Buy a chain for it, and get it ticking. I'd like to think the old thing's going to go again some time.'

A year later I had it mended, and bought a chain from a Polish watchmaker at the top of Drury Lane in Nottingham. I still wear it, and it keeps fair time. I never knew why Edgar's soul had been so much battered, and at times I disliked his better-off brothers intensely for not helping him more. They hadn't been exactly generous, and my father was all but ignored by them during his hard-up days. Only at Christmas did they give us a few toys left from the previous year. None of them came to my father's funeral, though an announcement had been put in the newspaper to give the date. Yet they had helped Edgar from time to time, and he usually sold or pawned the clothes they gave, spending the money on drink. So they got fed up and didn't bother with him.

He was knocked down by a bus and died alone in hospital at sixty years of age, worn out by his life. It was a miracle he survived so long.

57

The hardworking, self-righteous faction of the Sillitoe brothers – whom I shall lump under the generic name of Joseph – did not like the free-roaming, feckless Eddie nor the fly-by-night Frederick who called himself an artist. He considered these two, whom I give no common label because they were individuals right to the end, to be lax and rotten limbs of the clan. Fighting hard not to be like them, Joseph did not care to be reminded of their existence in case it impaired his upright resolution.

Despite Frederick's vicissitudes, and Edgar's hand-to-mouth life, they were thought to have it too easy. By similar standards my father should also have been disliked, but his unemployed state was considered to be no fault of his own, and in any case Joseph Sillitoe saw him as being backward in the head, and more to be pitied than blamed – as it was superciliously put.

I call these brothers 'Joseph' so as to cloak them under the anonymity of fiction, the only fashion in which truth can be protected against the inclement sky of fact. As a name it suits their common image, and because it came to me without thought I accept it to be pictorially true. Joseph of Genesis stood by his brothers in times of famine and stress, and so there is no connection between him and the present Joseph. But just as Joseph would not have been high lighted had his brothers never been born, neither would the composite Joseph Sillitoe have been at all vivid in his idiosyncrasies without the other three, less righteous males of the family.

Not that I'm drawing parallels. Two such lines do not meet even in infinity, and without a meeting there can be no truth. The only use of parallels is that you can see one from the other, and see it clearly, and in this alone they might be useful.

58

Eddie and Frederick should *know better*, Joseph thought. They realised all too well what they were on about, damn and blast them, but just didn't care to alter their ways, both to spite their family first, and to ruin themselves second. To Joseph they possessed Free Will, and he thought them wrong not to use it so as to dispossess themselves of it, as he had been forced to do.

It was not pleasant to see his own hidden yearnings given some benefit of liberation in others. Yet Joseph would have been unhappy with that freedom. He did not have the moral stamina to sustain such breadth, which therefore stopped him getting it, and which led him to condemn it in those who had got it – who in any case were not happy, though in his limited vision he did not realise this. It was better to condemn others, as a sure way of hiding his own faults.

There was a tight and lonesome streak in him, a need to stay by himself with what he had got, as if to be in life at all called for a sustained and painful effort. He wanted nothing more than to be left alone and looked after, like a baby still warm in the amniotic fluid. Even a neighbour knocking at the back door turned him into a tense, poised animal about to shout them abusively to hell.

Joseph fitted silently and resentfully into his occupation, grudging the near presence of his fellow-workers so much that in order to stay apart from them he laboured with a dedicated frenzy of industrious skill that made him invaluable to any customer or boss. Such an individualist was, of course, anti-social, paying no dues and joining nothing. If he had to buy a licence or fill in a form it was a wicked infringement of his personal liberty. A slight twist of humanisation might have made him a good anarchist, but for that slight twist to come about the planets would have to alter in their tracks.

Many might call him a typical Englishman, and if there was such a thing they could easily be right. Knowing the blood that ran in him I have always thought that an anti-social person was one hair's breadth from hating foreigners. He was certainly patriotic, for though he wasn't a 'joiner' he could always be persuaded to put on uniform in times of war. Without being loud about it he knew he must be patriotic because it would never do for his tight little world to be altered by any foreign or revolutionary influence. His safe cocoon might be upset. He might actually have to *meet* other people, people who were new to him what's more, strange people, the dark people, people not actually and absolutely like him, people who stood with their mouths open or who sweated when they worked, people who might not be as prepared as he was to leave everybody else alone – people, in fact, who might imagine they not only had a perfect and easy-going right to stop him in the street and ask the way to Sneinton Market, but also to talk to him about the weather afterwards.

And yet one must give him his due, for perhaps he thought,

152

with that modesty which is the opposite side of the coin to black conceit, that his soul was of value only to himself, and that he ought not to bother anyone else with it. A frustrated hermit, he suffered because he was forced to live through the muted agony of ordinary life, for which he did not feel himself fitted in any way, though he made a courageous attempt to go on with it.

He became so good at suffering in silence that the real wounded were those who were forced to live close to him, such as his own family, which served as a sort of lightning conductor. The pain of suppressed violence, emotional and otherwise, was etched on to the face of his wife and children, which enabled his set features to present a tight-lipped dignity to the world.

The real violence pent inside was sufficiently curbed by society, and he had the one good quality of being law-abiding, and therefore willing to allow society to influence him, in that by saving him from the realisation of his own wild and sombre fantasies it at the same time protected others. Providing the laws were good, he was reasonable, but if ever the laws became unjust to a certain portion of the community, and the law was on his side, he would be a demon.

At the same time, and to himself, he saw too much worth in his own soul. A man who overvalues his soul and nurtures it alone – pets it, indulges it, allows it to grow and get to full flower untampered as much as possible by society, who keeps it free and proud, and believes it to come straight out of the soil loving the wind and the smell of its own earth – is the hermit, the ascetic, the monument of selfish ecstasy, the bigot, and the patriot for himself alone.

He is the man who calls on God from his imprisoning parlour, which he sees as his very own and golden field and thinks is heaven on earth. But he would kill God if God appeared – after condemning him for lack of pride in condescending to approach a mere and lowly mortal such as himself. Calling to God in an ecstasy of self-approbation, the man in the middle of the field is too involved to help anybody. He has already given up hope of his fellow-men, which means that he never had any of God.

By way of an opposite we have the man who lives by the best of those moral laws inscribed in the various holy books of the world, the social man who interacts and confronts nature both as a communal act and to get his food. Such a man can be more tolerant and civilised, more sceptical and rational, and less dangerously dogmatical, a servant of God but not enamoured of the mystical soil, more religious in a family sense, and in a way more civilised. He would help a stranger as well as his neighbour. And he who helps a stranger will make sure his neighbour does not die alone. His brother certainly would not.

59

Joseph was dark-haired when young, and inclined to be stocky in middle age. Unlike the Burtons, who kept good heads of hair throughout their lives, he went bald by his late thirties, so that he was fairly pink on top when I knew him as a child. He had the eyes and forehead of a lawyer, or the discontented perspicacity of a manager in some provincial department store. His light-brown eyes betrayed the unrest within, indicating what great reserves of honesty were needed to control such potent turmoil. His fine sensitive fingers seemed to hold proof of the skill that saved him from himself.

He was a useful and talented craftsman, good with hands and eyes. Two of his brothers relinquished the family trade to become managers of butchers' shops, and on slack afternoons they would look forlornly at the traffic-flowing world over trays of chops and sausages, as if wondering how they came to be where they were, and whether they would ever get out of it except through the grave.

Joseph was a man of neither God nor Party, but if a man has no religion, one might ask, what then is left? His own soul, would be the reply. If a man has (in general) no patriotic feeling, what remains? His own country. If a man has no love to give, what can take its place? His own family. Their basic questions and answers could only have fallen out like that. And if the roots of Joseph's family were used and burned down for him there was only the sharp, debilitating, aching desire to find or meet some woman of cosmic force and passion to fall in love with who would alter everything. Death, life, death: in his dreams he saw a round-faced mature woman with reddish hair and small white teeth. Could that be anything to do with happiness?

Joseph and his brothers were non-men who had dragged themselves from the Welsh hills, or the misty marshes close by, and had made a go of it in Staffordshire because they could not go back to where they came from. Being not of this world they seemed to be more English than the Burtons, sole survivors of some lost tribe still too shattered by an unexplained disaster that had bitten at their tails.

Pride they had, but pride is a means of self-preservation when at bottom you are not sure of what there is to preserve. Or if you do have something to preserve then an excess of pride indicates that you feel yourself in danger of losing it. Pride is an encircling moat that you dig around yourself and fill with the muddy water of self-esteem.

Joseph was excessively proud and self-centred, and it was a for more concentrated pride than that of the Burtons, a meaner pride that not only drew the head back but also pulled in the stomach – which was just as well because Joseph was a rather sedentary and self-indulgent person. One felt that in order to get out of a tricky situation Burton would tell lies, while Joseph would tighten his face like jaundiced steel and grit his teeth as the leaden sky dropped in on him.

Burton was like a ramrod in his walk, born that way, it seemed, but Joseph was a turkey-cock who had to know he was proud, and constantly tell himself so, before he actually appeared proud to other people. His eyes then burned with the self-importance of the little man who believes he is the centre of the earth and of society around him.

He acted his part with panache, and a certain amount of

swagger, a show-off who is often recognised as the lynchpin and asset of a tight society afraid of falling to pieces. He was considered to be noteworthy and attractive enough, a by no means common attainment that lifted him – in his estimation – from the crowd round about. Where the Burtons might at most get stomach ulcers, the Sillitoes were prone to cancer.

As brothers they lived for themselves alone, not as a clan and for each other, but imprisoned in the airless cells of their families, which usually consisted of one or two children, except for my father, who was illiterate and had five. The fate of Joseph's wife would be a tale all of its own if he had not been so self-righteously discreet in his treatment of her. Full information rarely emerged.

Edgar's wife abandoned him to melancholia and idleness, and to his frequent tears brought on by memories of Gomme-court. The family always hoped for him: 'Then shall the eyes of the blind be opened, and the ears of the deaf unstopped,' – but they never were, because he retreated behind the safe palisade of his schizophrenia, and to the end of his life failed to shake it off.

Frederick left his wife after twenty years of marriage, to devote himself to art and freedom, though it may have been a mutual parting. An early scene of home-sweet-home is of my mother bending over a bucket to let the blood run into it after my father (a real Sillitoe, so the Burtons said) had used the usual overforce of his energy when he hit her on the head with a shoe.

What agony of the heart did he go through before the hand lifted to strike? I hope it lasted for a decently long time, though I suppose that after the first blow they came on call, almost with pleasure on both sides, as the barrier went down and the fist pounded. And if the pain of my father's soul seemed to have plagued him for an eternity before he picked up the shoe or clenched his fist, maybe it was really only a few minutes, in spite of how long it felt when he fought the great fight to leash back his vicious urges.

Joseph turned against women because, having an aversion for his own life, he held them to blame for his birth, unwilling to get up courage and turn such wrath on the father who was

156

equally responsible – or to set it at no one at all, but to do the impossible and live reasonably ever after.

He held his wife down more effectively than by knocking her about. He did it by sheer force of demonic personality. He oppressed her by oppressing himself even more, and there is no more final way of doing it than that. In other words, he did it at any price. He spited himself to crush his wife, and perhaps he thought it eminently worth while, since it held in check the parts of himself he was afraid of, but which were nothing more than the surviving freedom of his spirit which society had trained him to despise.

60

Joseph imagined that if he lived alone he would live longer, and that family life was cruelly shortening the number of his years on earth, time that would be blissfully untrammelled if he had no such domestic commitment. This fact, unjust to everyone, gnawed at his vitals. It was one of those fundamental untruths which had moulded his features – but became true after it had fixed them for ever. He could not know that if women want to stop living in the jungle with men, and if men care to ease their fang-and-claw existence with women, then they have to be together in peace, and start chopping the trees down instead of each other. Like most people, he could not see beyond the limits of his own conflict. If he could, it might no longer be there – and then what would he have to live for?

On his wedding day Joseph committed the minor and understandable fault of drinking too much whisky. When the guests left he turned on the wedding presents and smashed them to pieces. Or maybe it was something else, I'm not too sure. Whatever it was, it would have been easier on his wife if Joseph had been able to forget it. Then she might have forgotten it also.

But memory feeds on guilt, and guilt on memory. Without

memory there is no guilt: without guilt – no memory. Guilt attacks those least able to bear it, and who have done least to deserve it. It takes the energy of the weak who are trying to be strong. The monsters of history are immune to guilt. Those with long memories remember guilt till their dying hour. A harmless and repressed desire becomes an obsession that can turn into a crime, either quick and homicidal, or one that lasts forty years and leaves no obvious or open wound. So the women suffer more, because they are made to remember the wrong the husband is supposed to have committed by the continual phenomenon of his guilt, by which he leaves her in no doubt that he did whatever it was only because of meeting and marrying *her*. He implies that no one but she can be held responsible for it, though the nominal blame stays entirely his because he wants it that way, and won't let anyone forget it.

Guilt is that unacknowledged feeling at having come out of the slime, a useless sensation which drives the innocent into apathy and sloth. It begets the crime that creates another, and so it is compounded into a monstrous black tangle in the soul allowing no other person to live close by – unless they infect themselves with the same malaise, so as to be able to fight back and prevent themselves going dead under it. Joseph was guilty of nothing more than the harmless desire for a freer life. But he thought that to achieve it would utterly wreck his peace of mind, and maybe that of everyone near by, whereas in reality it would have liberated them as well, or at least made their lives more tolerable.

In a sudden rage he would hit the wall with his fist, while Burton, who did not recognise rage because he lost his temper far too easily, and who assumed absolute right to be on his side anyway, and who didn't need the fuel of guilt to get the best out of life, would hit his children. Is there much to choose between them? Joseph was bitter and timid. He lived in a twilight world of hard work and respectability, being the sort of person who decided early on in life that it was easier to pick up a cash book than a hod of bricks. He rarely worked hard enough for his labour to call forth much sweat, and even when he did, rather than mop his brow, he would stand and look as if he were bone dry, like someone not accustomed to sweating, in which case he would get dry sooner than if he took to wiping at the sweat assiduously – though he had the sort of skin that did not sweat much anyway.

He clung to his tight principles for fear he would drop into hell – hell being a chaotic place where he wouldn't be able to tell one person from another. He never made any contact with the Burtons, being geographically divided from them by the spiritual barrier of the Pennines – which assumed the same height and ruggedness as the Alps which cut off the Romans from the Numidians, until Hannibal pushed a way through the passes with elephants. Beyond the Pennines lay the flat, open lands of the Trent and the Fens, where the Burtons and all their like could stay for ever, part of that tribe of pikers who dealt in coneys and ponies and other such pastoral low life.

Joseph believed in the freedom of the individual in such a way that instead of being a slave to others he was a slave to himself. It was certainly a case with him that though self-pity corrupts, ordinary human pity corrupts absolutely because it would lead him into more contact with people. He would not get out into the world and compete with others. Competition was anathema and death, indignity and dishonour. He knew that safety lay in hard but ambitionless work, and with his combined qualities of tenacity, loyalty, application and skill he could appear proud without being put upon.

Though he was too sure of himself to compete, it was also true that he was riddled with envy. This was what stopped him competing, because with such a black dog on his back he could not be sure of success. So all he could do was hold down that envy with the jackboot of self-satisfaction.

There was a certain advantage to this exercise in repression. Knowing that envy was not a good trait, and that it ought to be resisted, he was able to take part in an honourable fight. This gave him a feeling of self-respect – which he might not otherwise have had, and which came by refusing to go into the common world and compete with it.

This absolute refusal to compete was in fact his strength. The inability to set himself against other men, to pitch himself into the jungle of ambition, to elbow his way up some shaky ladder of strife and success was his one saving virtue, no matter how it came about. If the coiled spring of his spirit had shot him across to America, or down to the Antipodes, he might have found such release from the English paralysis of class structure that he could have striven for a better life without being robbed of his dignity – as he felt he would have been had he tried the same thing at home.

61

My Uncle Frederick renamed himself *Silliter* when he came back to Nottingham in the thirties, in case his creditors of the previous decade should think to catch up with him. Fifteen years was not a long absence. The Market Place had changed, as had many of the buildings round about, but the prominent names of the stores he had, shall we say, *traded at*, told him that so many years might shrink to very few if a manager from one of them should spot him in the street.

Having been born a plain Church of England Christian, and spent twenty years as a Christadelphian, and then lapsed into atheism, Frederick had never shown much moral respectability to the community at large – no more perhaps than most people. But it seemed strange to me in my pre-sophistication days that, while priding himself on having learned Hebrew, he should have told one or two apparently anti-Jewish stories during the year or so in which I knew him. Perhaps they were rather too trivial to recall, because to be fair his words were harmless, in that they might have come after long association with Jewish colleagues who had made those same remarks in his presence. But at the time they were retailed to me (sheepishly, as I now recall, and possibly to test me) I could not be sure how serious he was. I also remember him stating, however – though he absolutely refused to elaborate – that 'the Jews taught me all I know.'

My father used to say, in a tone that combined both envy

and condemnation, that the Jews always helped each other. Much later in his life I heard him make a more open remark which shocked my Burton mother. I could not knock him down because one side of his head was dark from the bruises of cancer, and he died soon afterwards.

In life, when he was healthy, he loved me as a father prefers to love a son; when blinded and pounded by illness he would say anything to get some lasting effect from the world before he was forced out of it.

To forgive the dead is the first step towards illumination. In some ways it is easier, as well as more necessary, to understand the dead than the living, because the life of the dead is actually rounded off so that it becomes no more than a memory. They can neither disappoint nor deceive, but having existed they still live, and to comprehend their spirit one has to bring them back to a sharper portrayal than they were awarded while solidly moving. If you want them to return through the barrier they went beyond it is almost as if you have to go in and fetch them, get into their spirit and draw them out by an act of imagination and justice.

My father did too many kindnesses not to deserve forgiveness. He too had much to forgive, so that understanding was needed all round. What small harm he did was kept in his family, as society meant it to be, and he was never in a position to act out any of those poisonous hatreds which came from the Edwardian ethos in which he and his brothers had grown up. He was not anti-Semitic, because he did not possess that combination of intelligence and absolute narrow-minded scumbrained rottenness.

There were times though when he was anti-everything in his black despair, and my feeling is of sadness at his hard life, and for what was done to him by his parents. In such family conflicts one can neither withdraw nor take revenge. Savage or unthinking parents leave one merely paralysed, like an outsider.

In his tolerable moments he wanted to do good. When I was a child he got into debt to buy books for me, and money I gave when working later in a factory could never repay it. If you have seen your father suffer it is impossible to hate him, or to be afraid of him. The only thing you can do is try to understand, because not to do so will leave a large part of yourself in the wilderness. It is the same with others you dislike. You can never understand them, which means that much of yourself is lost to you, for you can only know yourself by knowing others.

In any case nothing attaches you more to a person than hatred. Those you hate have you more in their power than those you love. If you want to imprison someone in your own spirit, give them cause to hate you – and you have them for a long time, if that's how you feel. Universal and benign love would give everyone the greatest freedom of all, but people are unable to give this love because they are afraid of the freedom which is its price.

62

Just after the Second World War my father bought a bull-terrier. All his life he had wanted a dog, and in his middle forties he became the proud owner of one.

When he was walking up Ilkeston Road one day it snapped the lead and ran against a bus. It was fatally injured, and he came home weeping with it in his arms, as if it had been a child.

He laid it on a barrel inside the back door, and went for the vet, in the hope that the comatose and bleeding animal could be brought back to life. Yet any belief in miracles had gone from his heart generations ago. Tolerance of Biblical Job-like suffering had reasserted itself for a while during his middle years, but by now it was worn away because it did not have much moral strength to feed on. Faith in life had given way to sentimental hope.

When the vet came he jabbed a shot of pentathene into the dog's paw as it lay on the barrel. He talked to my father for a few minutes, putting him wise as to where he might get another dog, and also to calm him down. Then he gave the dog a dose of strychnine which finished it off.

My father didn't buy another dog. Never having got out of the nursery, as it were, there was only room for one woman in his life, no matter what the pain. And there was only room for one dog as well, as representative of a certain kind of creature, so that he could not start again on another. It would not be the same.

One of his favourite pictures was taken from a calendar. It was a coloured reproduction photo of a young woman standing at a cottage window on a sunny day in the country. She wore a yellow dress, and had a girl of about three years of age in her arms. They were looking together at a robin perched on the branch of a tree close by, both of them warm and loving with each other, and enraptured at the bird.

My father liked this picture. Such a scene went straight to his heart. It stayed there, a sort of imprint of paradise which he neatly framed with black passe-partout tape and hung on the wall, and took from house to house when we moved. He liked it because he identified with the little girl in the woman's arms – certainly not with the woman herself, or with the bird.

PART THREE

63

The River Leen was sinewy and narrow, though its Celtic name of 'lleven' also suggests 'smooth-surfaced'. But the root of the word may be 'linn' meaning 'still, deep pool', and it certainly is that in places. Whenever I heard the phrase 'still waters run deep' either about me or somebody else, I always flashed my picture-mind to the River Leen, whose water I would recently have looked on from the brick parapet of the bridge. While playing on its steep bank I once fell into it from an imperfect balance on the bough of a tree, and though its waters were not still they certainly stank, having come through mills and collieries most of the way from Robin Hood's hills near Mansfield.

Early expeditions over the fields to the Burtons at Engine Town took me across the River Leen, and then a railway which ran along its shallow, wide valley. These two obstacles both hemmed me in and tempted me out, and made the advance beyond into an adventure of the spirit, as well as an exploration of new territory.

Crossing the railway I would sit on the fence by its side, watching coal-trains pulling trucks from Nottinghamshire collieries. In those days before the mines were nationalised I read the names painted broadly and plainly on each truck as it went by, one strange word after another, some so quick and difficult that I had to see them several times before my memory held them. Nevertheless, the words came fast, forming an eternal telegram that was never sent, but which still occasionally spins into my head:

165

BOLSOVER
ALDERCAR
TIBSHELF
NUNCARGATE
CLIPSTON
PLEASLEY
NEWSTEAD
PINXTON
TEVERSAL
BLIDWORTH
RIDDINGS
HUTHWAITE

romantic place-labels, almost as if they had come from Italy or
Abyssinia, and while they showed me the headstocks of their
collieries, like the one I could see just up the line, I did not
also visualise – as I no doubt should have done but am pleased
I did not – row upon row of miners' houses that would be
clustered round about. Or if I did, they were set in the sunshine
of hilltop situations, and were altogether more picturesque and
salubrious than those among which I lived.

I recited their names like a litany for the rest of my way to
the Burtons, as I broke through hedges and leapt streams.
They kept me company when the sky darkened and it began to
thunder. I remember the smell of bacon frying on damp Sunday mornings in summer. And when I slept at the Burtons' on
Saturday night, those big white words on the coal trucks rode
by in my dreams.

The stuff and fibre of people's language is made up of
names. Total history is nothing less than an accounting of
every name in it – not just a few, but all of them. Without a
name nothing exists – neither place, person, nor piece. Names
cement the regions and generations in such a way that time
becomes timeless, and only words are important, the labels
that pinpoint a person's soul, the backdrop and bedrock of
language.

Names mean life and matter that is always on the go. They
decay and change, fret and vanish, then come up somewhere
else and grow again. Those who hold their names too tight

get buried with them – just as raindrops, glorying too much in their own moisture, melt on meeting soil.

Names remain. The passing years pile up and give them tales and weight, or bleed them white and take out all significance. When you can't tell one name from another all men look the same. The more people there are, the more you know them by their names or not at all. An increase in breeding broadens the tongue. We must know one from another – man and name – if civilisation is to take hold and properly accumulate true richness.

When the wild and conquering hordes settled down to their fields they contemplated each other and gave out names that would last. A cycle is complete and now stands. Poets take over. Tillage and metre rule. The seasons and the moon dominate utterly when every place and person has a name – some of which eventually ride by on coal trucks through disordered childhood dreams.

64

When I told my father I was going to have a novel published he said: 'That's bloody good. You'll never have to work again' – as if I'd been given a million pounds in exchange for colic on the heart. Twenty books later I still see what he means. 'You've got an aim in life now,' he added, though with more truth than before.

But to write books is not to have an aim in life. It is a camouflage under which a real aim can wither before it is even understood. By blind chance I became a writer, and unknowingly sidestepped a career which might have turned out more useful and satisfying. It is a futile thought that occasionally flashes in, but as long as my proper fate stays with me – as it presumably does – I shan't complain.

Any true aim perished in the blinding light of emptiness

when I tried to understand it, and so my spirit withdrew from the struggle as if it were burned, and took refuge in the greater comfort of the periphery, where the process of writing begins. And if in spite of this I still mull on it and wonder why I became a writer, I'm careful not to make the mistake of driving straight to the empty middle and search for the truth there.

Having sorted among the aborted tributaries of my family it is no use coming back into the core of myself to get at the truth. It would be a sentimental head-on clash, to be avoided at all costs. It is better to chase the indirect and apparently unimportant as being more worthwhile, to keep my thoughts clear and insignificant, rather than boringly definitive.

In someone of low intelligence sentimentality is pathetic. In those of high intelligence it is obnoxious, even dangerous. I will not decide which of these categories I fit into, but state them so as not to get entangled – and send one into that great central fire of emptiness where they can burn into gas and ashes, while I stay on the rich outside.

A writer is born without God, and his centre has been taken over so that he is a god. It could be that he then spends his life writing in order to hold off the fear of dying and death, and keeps writing so as not to expose himself to the danger of having his questions answered and therefore of having to accept God.

The ultimate aim is to phrase questions, not to solve them, for if you show people what to ask, they will soon find their own solutions. A question is not a question unless it contains the seeds of its answer, and when this phenomenon occurs to a primitive or uneducated person he overcomes his fear of the world and makes a fundamental break with his past. For a writer, another sort of fear comes with the questions, because he is afraid that the questions may desert him. It also stays because fear is a birthmark of life. Those who do not have it are not yet born. Whoever says 'I am not afraid' has grown old before his time. Who cannot suffer morally, perishes physically. Lack of fear bursts the heart, which is the worst of diseases. If the bravest of the brave replies that fear makes the face ugly, and takes all honest beauty from it, and that the earth will despise the fearful and pull him more quickly to his death, he is wrong. To be fearful is to be able to love. To lie three days in no-man's-land as Edgar did, with every minute full of terror from the rats, men, and unseen dismemberment, was a feat of adoration for the scarred earth he clung to. It was a love that drove him almost out of his mind, a state of question without answer he chose to live with for the rest of his life.

The soil also pulls you under out of love, and since death is the end it is better for it to be welcoming than ward you off. It will cool and cushion those who are hot from dying, or merely warm you if the chill of crossing that terrible barrier is still present.

65

A simple man is a person who cannot express his complexities. A writer expresses them for him and still lets him keep the illusion of his simplicity. The Burtons are the simple men in me, but they had illusions of complexity that could never break out. The Sillitoes are the complex men, but they had illusions of simplicity that could not prevent the complexities from tormenting them.

The qualities of one family shift on to the other. They merge and cross-fertilise, become a running sore, ruining memory in a sea of psychic pain – which I distrust. Truth is like the tip of an iceberg: one-tenth of it based on nine-tenths lie. When I am out walking I sometimes feel the sallow Sillitoe backness gaining the upper hand over the optimistic, energetic, easygoing Burton lot. At such times the two forces separate, and leave me in the middle of an expanding emptiness.

The past is fiction, what bits of it can be remembered. The present is illusion, what pains of it can be felt. Only the future exists, because it is yet to happen. When it does, it also is full of flickering uncertainties impossible to latch on to, so that with necessary speed it fades into the fiction of the past. Yet out of this past which has become fiction I fish for the truth, and even knowing a great deal about my grandparents, it is impossible to say for certain where I come from, or where I belong. A man only knows he comes out of his mother, and has to be satisfied with that. To dispute it and want to believe otherwise means to accept the maxim that emotion is tempered by reason – before conclusions can be drawn.

But emotion tempered by reason is a perfect excuse for pride of place and faint-of-heart. Emotion, it is true, smothers reason. And reason emasculates emotion. The uneasy combination, if ever it is achieved, is the very body of reaction. If reason goes forward like the patrols of an advancing army, emotion in full body catches up to wield its destructive victory. If the emotional vanguard goes on ahead, reason eventually overtakes and robs it of any achievement. Sooner or later, reason and emotion rend each other, and leave a desert. They are terms of mutual annihilation. Is this emotion? Or is it reason? A jointure of the two makes it no better. Both reason and emotion are too near the surface to be properly controlled and matched.

As if born in a state of spiritual decapitation a writer wants to join his head back on to his body, the Scipio on to the Africanus, the first name on to the second, to sew the soul into the stomach and throw them together into the river of life, there to rend each other, to sink or swim. Perhaps he only succeeds in unifying himself when he is about to die, by which time it is too late. He fears death because it means that his life as an earthly god will come to an end. And if after life there is still more life, there can be no more final death for a writer.

If anything exists in the burning middle it is an alchemical brazier of the soul, driven white by a salt wind coming from the sea. Both gale and blaze thrive on each other and never let go. In the storm's centre I ask myself what I am, but cannot say. Forty days or forty years can be spent in the attempt, but if one doesn't know without even asking, then all further tries are bound to collapse.

Yet the more unsuccessful, the fuller in spirit one becomes, the greater the overall richness of life will be. If I look in a mirror and ask this question I get a blank look, or enough of a shocked expression to remind me that it is not a question but a riddle. The half-smile that lingers in the mirror after I have turned my head tells me that I still have a sense of humour, which is the last defence against the truth.

To go bull-headed at the riddle means I'll never get an answer. I am a writer because I do not know what or who I am, though in trying to find out I may by a fluke help others to know who they are. If so I trust it will persuade them to go on living and not despair about the fate of the world or themselves.

You have to go beyond the limits of despair to reach the truth. Certainly you cannot get close to it by standing still, or by locking yourself into an idiot-gaze against the warm and comforting fireplace. You move a finger, stare at the hand and lift it with a movement of the arm, and then you stand up and feel the pressure of the ground in both legs, and you shift across the room and look through the window and go to the door and open it and walk outside to smell the sky and let the wind into the brain. The senses waken as the odour of fields and marshes rushes in. While gleaning for the truth, despair calls from one side and hope beckons at the other, and they try and draw you apart. When such horse-mares struggle for your inner vision you manage to walk, or take a spade and dig the soil over.

To be without hope, in the belief that nothing is worth living or working for is an act of murder against the human spirit, self-willed or not. One must learn to suffer without taking to despair, for despair is a killer, a suicide-monger, the mongrel-devil who does not hand out any consolation, even in death. Yet if those who fall into this trough have no control against being brought to it, they are in a state of grace and waiting to be saved. The axis of the world's goodness depends on them, and upon those with the strength and will to help.

The sphere of white fire spins, an illumination of truth which can never be reached simply by wanting to. I use it to see by. It dazzles and blinds when I reach out and try to use it: it uses me. Art is order made out of chaos; false art is chaos made out of the false order already in existence.

If I am to go forward I must switch round and get free of the cul-de-sac, otherwise I do violence to the soul. There is a part of every book which turns out to be a dead-end, and you need sooner or later to reverse from it. I entered this one on a trip into the past, and to reach clear space once more I must fight against all the purples of the spectrum.

Geometry exists so that the fringes of chaos can be surveyed, and the remotest zones of confusion explored and classified. All mysteries are encountered, but few have their meanings revealed, and even then they cannot be understood. The route pencilled on the map is like a question-mark upside down.

66

The conscious and the subconscious come twice in the same sphere, and Man's soul is as complete as the zones and seasons of the earth.

There is a consciousness in the northern hemisphere hemmed in by the cold subconscious of the Arctic, and by the subconscious of the heat between Cancer and the Equator.

There is a consciousness in the southern hemisphere bounded by the subconscious of the Antarctic ice and the subconscious of the tropics between Capricorn and the Equator.

Thus there is more than one consciousness, and more than one subconscious. There is a consciousness trapped between the heat and cold of the northern hemisphere. There is a consciousness caught by the heat and cold of the southern hemisphere.

There is a consciousness and a subconscious and in both the northern and southern hemispheres of the earth and of the soul.

Under this vast conscious-subconscious crust is the seething reservoir at the centre of man's earth-soul that fuses both the conscious and the subconscious, and from which all the facets of the personality emerge – or do not, depending on how it is treated.

Consciousness holds itself between ice and heat, the Pole and the Equator in both north and south. My subconscious is of the ice and finally frozen too deeply to become tractable. My subconscious is of the tropics, and only rarely cools itself enough to be understood. The consciousness in both cases keeps the two walls of the subconscious apart. The subconscious in both cases wants to cross over the zones of the consciousness and meet, but the integuments of the consciousness prevent this. At the same time it wants to pull in the subconscious on to itself, but though it may wish to draw them together in a merging of the whole, this is impossible unless one's consciousness has the equivalent in spirit of Samson's super-human strength – who was said to be so strong that he could uplift two mountains and rub them together like two clods of earth.

This is the universe of the shaman, the geography of fire and ice, the equating of strength in the arm with air that comes out of the mouth. The conscious zone between the borders of the subconscious is a region both turbulent and temperate, fragile and sensitive, prone to freeze with the ice or melt with the heat. The membranes of the heart can burst because of an increase of one degree, or split when it goes down a shade, the sensitive zone that draws all the subtleties of chills and fevers, fits and miseries, screams and dreams against it, tissues through which everything can be learned, and in which one feels the grail and mystery one clings to for fear of falling down the side of the earth and going still living into the blackness.

Thus the conscious, that which is supposed to be on top and in sight – the obvious; and the subconscious, that which is hidden and of which we are not often aware – the unknown and menacing. They have their own geography, not the normal top-and-bottom Freudian kind that I might have learned to live with if I had not been born to search after my own truth, but a more complicated, geopsychic flux of forces, of a globe whose maps show a constantly shifting tectonic surface.

This chart of the soul indicates that the ultimate truth will never show itself, no matter how long the search goes on. To penetrate one subconscious is difficult, but to cut a way into two is not feasible. One moment they help each other, the next minute they compete and intermix, hinder and pull apart.

The double meeting of ice and heat generate their own phosphorescence, a forked illumination from two batteries, twin sources of power. Though one light makes for clarity, two create confusion. They cross-dazzle and blind, and closing the eyes in order to escape it only sends you back into the dark, in which the heat fights the cold in an eternal battle of opposites.

From this prism of the soul grows understanding. This system of the conscious and the subconscious increases confusion. There is a purpose in everything. It is either an excuse for not being able to get at the truth, or it is done in the belief that truth can only be pulled from chaos, not from the false truths already in existence. Having a subconscious in the ice of the northern pole, and another in the intense heat of the Equator, I am able to draw on more than one consciousness, and be fed by more than one subconscious. One hemisphere of the conscious – subconscious is inhabited by the Sillitoe ethos, and the second contains that of the Burtons. The devils of both fight the angels of both.

This might be sure proof of madness – if I believed in madness, which I do not. It is said that someone who is mad has so many souls in the greater soul that he is unable to control them properly. They heave and push, like the hemispheres closing in, and one soul hasn't the knack of playing off the other as it has in a person who can contain them.

The circle never breaks. It explodes from time to time and takes us forward, but constantly reforms. Chaos is the source of life and richness. Order is not possible without chaos. It is the combustible charge that energises the arteries of the mind. Through such raw material one can travel back to anyone and any condition, and forward without fear into another chaos, to touch the heat of more raw material for a moment before returning laden with this loot of the spirit.

One must do it without fear, and to get rid of fear one needs to find the truth. The nearer we get to the truth, the further away it is. Like trying to reach the most distant star of the universe, there will always be another beyond it. Our fingertips are not made of the right stuff to touch the end of all experience, nor our wide-open eyes to see it. We can only put forward stepping stones to extend the limits of our understanding into as many colours and complexities as it will take without being crushed in on itself, set a compass towards infinity, but not into it; go in the pursuit of truth but never get close enough to touch it.

67

I sit and write at a somewhat unstable table with one of Burton's horseshoes in front of me, and Edgar's open-faced Gommecourt watch to keep the time. The third and small hand on the dial of it pushes the seconds behind as it hurries on an endless donkey-like journey into the future. There's no doubt about the truth of that.

The table is old and rickety, found in the garage among lots of rubbish abandoned by the last people who lived here, but I like its large rough surface on which I spread notebooks and papers, ashtray, inkwell, and bric-à-brac lavishly. It is dangerously active with splinters, but I can spill ink over it with impunity, and it stretches the whole length of the double window, to face trees and bushes beyond.

It is inevitable that I should wind back to my workroom in a quiet country house – not always silent when a gale blows as if to bump it flat. To spend the time trying to write I have my playthings of gramophone and tape-recorder. On another table is a high-powered black and magic box of a wireless receiver that weighs 60 kilos and can barely be carried from the removal van at each change of house. An ex-service communications set, it brings in wonderfully clear and amplified morse so that I listen to wireless-telegraph stations, and write down telegrams from ships to see if any information suggests a story or poem.

It never does, of course, though it is a relaxing pastime. A

175

100-foot wire running up the side of the house and across the garden to a tree helps me to hear Peking or Australia, Japan or the Voice of Zion from Jerusalem – loud and clear – giving the illusion of being in touch with the world.

The mechanical effect of taking morse at telegraphic speed persuades me I could still be useful as a radio-operator. Even though trained for it over twenty years ago I read it as fast and accurately as ever. Perhaps I come from families where economy of sweat and effort was paramount, and nothing taken in as a trade or job should be wasted, because it might one day come in handy and show its value again. However it was, the basic morse rhythms never left my brain, and I don't suppose they will, having been programmed on to it. The symbols for certain letters being absolute facts, maybe I am attracted by it for this reason. The alphabet has a sound rhythm, a drumbeat construction as it cuts through the ether and forces my brain to change it into words, makes my hand decipher it like a form of magic, which it is though, as with all magic, it is only the result of prolonged learning. At dusk, when birds send out territorial and mating calls, I hear their sounds as morse signals. Each bird has its own set letter of the alphabet going like a superheterodyne spark among the long shadows.

After nightfall and the curtains are drawn I can switch on and listen to Mendelssohn or Prokofiev, Mozart or Shostakovitch or Elgar, or the rich and sombre voice of Chaliapin singing his peasant songs and arias. There is also a record given to me in Russia, with Tolstoy reading a few paragraphs of *War and Peace*, and Yesenin and Mayakovsky reciting their poems, and Maxim Gorki giving a speech. Though I only understand a few words, their spirits fill the room.

A small rack of treasured and personal books includes a copy of the Bible given to me before the assembled school for 'proficiency in Biblical knowledge'. I was embarrassed at having to go up and get it, but it is a volume with a fine soft leather cover which I always have with me. Years ago I tore out the New Testament and threw it away, but now I have the Holy Scriptures from the Masoretic Text so that I can read it through from Genesis to Second Chronicles in the right order. I have read the old books several times, and prefer their poetry to the Christian part, leave myself with a thousand pages of great verse, from the awesome openings of Genesis to the ultimate words of the Prophets, an exhalation of life to comfort me through all existences.

Other titles in my bookcase of specialities are dictionaries by Skeat and Halliwell, Isaac Taylor and Bardsley; as well as Mackay's *Extraordinary Popular Delusions* and a couple of works on the history and topography of my home county. The dozen or so publications of my own I keep well away, not because I have anything against them, but I don't want to be reminded of their existence while I'm writing something new, so that I can treat each book in progress as if it's my first novel.

Apart from bookshelves, the wallspace shows maps like beds of flowers, a street plan of Nottingham, a large-scale trench-map of the Gommecourt salient in 1916, marked by the advancing death-lines of the Sherwood Foresters, a relief chart of Deception Island, and a topographical map of Israel flanked by the Mediterranean and the Jordan River, topped by Mount Hermon and bottomed by the southern arrowhead of Sinai – different regions I cannot shut my eyes to.

Books and life and maps and ink, and time to write and think and dip in my pen before pulling it across the paper with my left hand: can any truth come out of that? A writer writes what he likes, and it is vital that he does so – anything from theology to pornography, from politics and comics to sapphics and classics – no matter what world-system he lives under. Every man's truth is his own secret, but the only secret he can afford to have is that he has no truth.

68

Feckless Celts wandered across the face of Europe from the Caspian over the Carpathians, from Bavaria to Brittany, only to be pounded into a dull and baffled astuteness when they reached Albion, from which they soon lost the will to get free but not the picturesque desire to do so.

I was surprised to read a recent newspaper article in which some true-blue English person was quoted as saying that as far as she was concerned all Celts were foreigners. Being more than half Celt I thought there might be some truth in it. Indeed I hoped there was, for such a way-out Little English idea could explain the yearning for travel I have often too plainly felt – the need to get away from it by rail, road, or even bicycle, to walk out on foot if the worst came to the worst.

The pictures reflected in the eyes of Joseph and his brothers were of landscapes not people. Their religion was freedom, but because society totally stamped on it they could only worship in secret, like a resistance movement that had lost all hope, as if realising that direct access to the life they craved would blow them either to pieces or into paradise. When the raw material started to eat its own raw material they would move, but somehow their courage never allowed them to start chewing. Freedom pointed in the wrong direction, and their lack of courage became a means of self-preservation. They needed to communicate with themselves but had no way of achieving it.

The generous and lecherous spirit of the eighteenth century, crushed for more than a hundred years by the descending death-trap ceiling of tight-arsed Victorian hypocrisy and repression, is at last trying to break free. It did not begin in Joseph's life, though his melancholia came from thinking it was time to start pounding off the lid, but not being able to.

At school I was once taunted as a foreigner because my name was thought to be Italian. I did not mind this, though fought successfully against it since I refused to be humiliated for any reason. My father's idea that the family way back in time had come from Italy was only another of his flights of fancy – for in fact my surname came from Iceland. And yet if I were split down the middle by God's axe let us suppose that the Celtic or whatever part of me would happily turn into the Eternal Wanderer and walk purposefully away, glad to get out of this island and into the wide world before all Celts were rounded up and marched off to the gas chambers.

178

In a way I was flattered by the woman's remark. Having wanted to leave home and country almost from the cradle I nurse a secret ambition to be a foreigner, to become a man without nationality or passport but with the freedom to drift wherever I wanted. Shed of all ties and connections I would go my way alone on the travel-lanes of the world, a ghost of selfishness wallowing in so much land he eventually sees no people in it, and whom in turn nobody sees, a man so gripped by his infatuation for the form and smell of the earth that all love goes from him except inordinate fondness for himself.

It is an impulse to be resisted, though to desire such freedom is innocent enough because it keeps me imprisoned in an inner turmoil conducive to the act of writing. That is one way of doing it, after all. On the other hand, to actively pursue that vast and empty form of liberty would be an escape route into the death of the soul. Such a release from the anchored spirit could be done as a religious exercise perhaps, but since I am not one of the faithful it would turn it into an act of negation. My main purpose on earth is to be myself, which means getting closer to people, not away from them.

I circle around and spiral down, conjuring more dreams out of myself, numberless demons, becoming more empty, or more calm. If I believe my spirit is formed by my parents and their families – plus that alchemical mixing that can never be explained – the zig-zag switch-about for truth must go on, not to fill the emptiness of which I am not afraid, but so that the more void the emptiness becomes the more alive it gets with that potent electricity of the mind that keeps a person free of cant, lies, and tyranny.

When the different streams of my grandparents come flowing in I feel indeed that I am the product of a mixed marriage, the crux of two merging deltas, and if I ask in this white heat why I became a writer I say that the poetry comes out of the Burton side of the family, while the force that pushes it through is drawn from my father's.

Everything which concerns these various relations has some truth, whether or not I was directly involved in it. To detail the sum of these items is a circuitous way of pointing out traits which might bear on my own half-buried character, and with this in mind it is impossible to say which particular person I favour or 'take after', though I plainly attached myself most to those who had some skill and knowledge to impart: to Frederick the designer and artist, and to Burton the farrier.

69

Deception Island lies in a particularly eruptive area of the Antarctic Ocean and is all that remains of a volcanic cone suddenly pulled under by some insufferable whim of the earth. Most of it, except for whaling buildings and a scientific station, is composed of mountainous ash and ice, peaks, crevices, and sheer walls dropping into the sea.

The crater is not quite a full circle of land. It is broken at the mouth, part of its lip having gone with the general subsidence, leaving a gap so that its final shape is of a distorted horseshoe – a long way from the perfect specimen done by Burton in his prime which presses down the pile of written sheets on my table.

As unpredictable as a volcano, Burton created a primeval shoe-tool for the sacred horse, with iron that had been scraped out of the earth itself. Taking his piece from the fire he pounded the burning ore and made sparks live and die, plying his weight over the shape it was going to be. As he gripped the tongs and held his hammer, no thought entered his mind to spoil the meeting of anvil and nascent horseshoe. They came together with the built-in skill of his craft, producing an object he would set against the finest of any other smith.

During the Great War, when meat was scarce, Burton would not eat the horse-flesh which was sold in the shops, nor allow it into the house. The idea of it horrified his family as well, as if to consume such meat was little different to cannibalism. He loved horses, having in his trade learned to control them more thoroughly than any woman. His hatred of the canine

180

species (above all other animals) may have been because the dog was once a wolf, and the mythical enemy of both horse and man.

When man tamed the horse, blacksmiths made iron shoes for it, drove the nails in through seven holes for each foot, making twenty-eight all told – one for every day of the complete moon – that the horse pressed to the earth as a testament to man's dependence on the soil and the glowing guardian of the night sky.

Blacksmithery was a deified trade, honoured by Vulcan and Tubal-Cain. When he made sparks fly a blacksmith was said to be in touch with the underworld, risking his soul by working in iron and having traffic with the Devil. Thus the blacksmith can be related to poets, who are also in thrall to moon, earth, and underworld, and consume themselves utterly by the medium of their work.

The horseshoe on my desk is a well-made artefact of seven holes for seven nails, and my consciousness tames the wild horse that the junction of the two disparate psyches lets loose in me. Seventy years later the horseshoe Burton made lies heavy and cold, its perfect form pressing down the phrenetic scrapings from the back of a brain that Burton would never have connected himself with – aphorisms, observances, slick clippings, stray poems, and fragments that could not have come from anywhere except out of a Burton.

Passed on to me, the horseshoe of his spirit is as misshapen as the map of Deception Island pinned to my wall.

70

Burton's horseshoe holds down the notes and mulch-thoughts that come to me at midnight and after. One says that a writer is an old man who picks up a pen instead of garrulously speaking his words into thin air. If in need of a certain sort of painkiller he bites on words instead of bullets. I was a premature old man as a child, which is one reason why Burton and I hit it off so well together. A writer has no age but old age, though he only becomes senile if he stops writing, and when that happens he usually finds some way to die, no matter how old he is.

Vanity inscribes such secret thoughts, but they are a way of formulating the frequent question as to why one became a writer. The pile of papers underneath the horseshoe may provide a clue to this elusive puzzle: I can see it as a grand travelling trunk of raw material, and me lifting the lid occasionally to make a lucky dip or pick a winning number out of the raffle-bag.

No writer should take drugs, it says, or drink too much, or get psychoanalysed. Such things are for the others. If he feels himself going mad it is only part of the creative process – the soul rebelling at some offence against the sacred code, or showing a new direction for his talent. Madness is to be welcomed, and shared with no one.

A writer's reality is other people. His hell is himself, whom he is continually trying to get away from, or explain into extinction. But he cannot escape, because the long exploration which lasts all his life, from *alef* to *tav*, takes him deeper into that skin-enclosed world of visionary shade and colour, badger-runs of memory and all inventions of the soul. He goes to find out what is there, and organise it into any sense he can. From such material he creates his *golems* and sends them on to the sidewalks.

Close to heaven and hell, the writer paces a narrow lane between the frontiers of both, with a passport for neither place. To sidestep his own demon by choosing one or the other means death. A writer is a born and sometimes eloquent loser – a person who cannot win. He is never satisfied with what he does because he is always trying for the impossible, to remake himself according to a dream of perfection that he felt close to since birth, and to keep himself as alive as the language which surrounds him. He is attacked continually by his basic self, and so is forced into a never-ending quest for the truth by which he can be remoulded into the ideal man – meaning the most ordinary of men.

The impulse behind his endeavour is one of gnawing un-certainty, which would not leave him alone even if by a miracle he finished his task. So he compromises, tries to de-lineate an emotion or experience beyond the limits of what he had done before, to make reality out of a dream, to turn a vision into ordinary experience, to think complicated and write plain, to re-fabricate life and construct people because he cannot take himself to pieces like a clock, and find out what makes the world go.

He became a writer because there was no other way out of the dilemma, which in any case was insoluble. There is no single explanation. The feeling of being a born loser turned him into the only endless direction that was open, so he began to write and accepted the role of scapegoat and sacrifice, fate's potlatch, doomed never to tackle the fundamental problems of his life or finally explain them.

To make his existence supportable he finds it easier to tackle the despair of others than mend his own disabilities. This binds him tightly to humanity. His attempts to write instead of perish help to keep him and the world sane, give people something to live for, provide them with a fragment of hope in a desperate planet when they might otherwise think that universal extinc-tion is the answer.

Too many occurrences of actual life rob him of time which would be better spent writing, though to use this as an ideal merely brings down the troubles he hopes to avoid. There is no way out of that one, but the argument that experience widens his spirit is false. In the beginning his spirit is a door, which opens more and more of its own accord as be gets older. A writer has to go further back than that. He should match the suffering of others with his fresh imagination, mix in with his tribulations, and illuminate the fused result with that third and holy eye which not only guards the past as he goes forward but also watches for treachery from it, keeping it clear and well balanced in his own iron-wrought truth.

71

Being a writer is the one great fact, my only love, a love which I had to feel before I could fall in love with anything or anyone else. It had to be there even before I could fall in love with myself.

I can only write about people I love, even if they are crooks, cowards, scoundrels, weaklings, and renegades whom the rest of society abominates. The evil and the cynical in me also has its favourite characters which it likes showing to others. One falls in love with that which can either destroy or save, knowing that in the end there will be no difference between either state of the brain or backbone.

At the beginning I felt an air of mystery and importance at being a writer – of hardly caring whether I was a writer or not, because an inner fire that I hadn't yet uncovered but which kept me faithful to it knew that I was and would be, no matter what happened. It was pure and naïve enthusiasm, a feeling of youthful love that did not come and go in a month or year but went on like real love till it turned underground in order to survive. Like real love it is still there, and always will be, but I can never forget the time when it made me happy, in spite of all adversities and turmoil, just to tell myself that I was a writer, even though ten years were to go by before anything was printed. If any other person detected it they might have thought it was because I was in love.

To lose one's naïvety is to say good-bye to part of one's soul. Youth has vanished, leaving an ashen disaster. If enthusiasm in its first rush is cut down by the sword of cynicism, or by reality, or common sense, or critical praise, or reviewers' dislike, or an acceptance of any truth, it is a great misfortune, and wrong indeed to allow it. A writer is open, vulnerable, a prey to derision, and it is good for him that he says so, otherwise he will never get respect from those who matter to him, nor any from himself. Those who clamour for nothing but the truth, who demand easy and unconsidered opinions as well as form and style and deadly academic care, only want to spread his guts out in the sun to see what he is made of. They scatter sawdust over his remains with gestures of disgust when they see that he is built the same as everyone else except them.

The great poet David had a verse for it, when he realised the true nature of man's most sacred possession: 'Let them be ashamed and confounded that seek after my soul: let them be turned backward, and put to confusion that desire my hurt.'

A writer must search for the integral large space of his soul and, once he has found it, never abandon it, and be always sure to write with his own true voice, and not reflect the shallow guidelines of society. If there comes a time when he cannot distinguish between the two, then he should no longer call himself a writer. He must break through the thin gauze of the social fabric and get to what exists underneath, to that which has more meaning. It may not be easy to pick out the truth, but it is not difficult to distinguish the lies. If a writer is awarded some form of authority by the society in which he lives, and he believes in that authority, he loses blood, and indulges in artistic suicide. He slits his wrists in the warm bath of society's approval, and dies with a flaccid smile on his face.

No writer should agree to the simplicities and deceptions of the society in which he lives, and if he is true to himself he must fight against bourgeois culture, communist or otherwise, for with its lifeboats of surrealism and socialist realism it is a culture of deadness and mediocrity, sadism and self-praise imposed by those who came into the world with the truth on their lips and with nothing human in their hearts.

Some writers cannot go below the skin of their perceptions, so keep within standard lines of behaviour, and stick to the fossilised social patterns created for them. Others use the imagination as a way of exploring chaos, employing examples of archetypal myths that belong to both the past and the future. A writer may not be popular in this, but he is brought near the edge of sanity on beginning to write. His mind splits, becomes fragmented, and creates an agony which forces his pen to move in an attempt to reassemble it and so attain the peace of putting on paper what did not exist before. He is driven up to the holy frontier by the barbs of madness, but once there he is serene, writing with honesty and fire, and as near the truth as he can get.

72

If the writer is to preserve his integrity and inspiration he must be concerned with life beyond such public arenas as the boxing ring or the cockpit, out of range of groans or cheers from people who are in thrall to such anaesthetical comfort. They are beguiled by a brash and clamorous truth which is not theirs, truth which is too much in the present, and exploits them because it is somebody else's. Purveying what it believes to be the basic truths of the people, it deliberately puts them out in a monstrously exaggerated fashion, thus pampering the people into a sort of craven inanition, or a self-satisfying acceptance of all their vices. It stuns their senses, and no one can deny that they like its tune, for it takes them away from their own realities, which are less intoxicating, and more troublesome to all concerned.

How far must one go in fighting those who believe in the white truth, the absolute truth, their especial creed by which they seek to enslave others and force them into a ruination of their dignity? A writer can only live by his own truth if he is able to exist without offending his moral conscience. Otherwise he must fight, and in battling to preserve the integrity of the artist, he struggles to maintain the freedom of all individuals. This is another truth I will accept, but though I keep it small so that it tyrannises no one, I hope to keep it big enough to fight all tyranny. You can only contend against unjust laws by breaking the law. There is no other way. Most

186

laws are not made for the smooth running of society, but to keep people unnecessarily docile. Society could run itself, but those in power make laws, and thereby impose a tyranny which seeks to fix everyone in his place. Such domination destroys energy, talent, and any tangible freedom.

The great virtue of the English (especially the so-called lower classes) is that they are still expected to know their place in the social hierarchy created for them. The simple English workman is much honoured if he stays where he belongs. But it is not like that any more. Nowadays he is beginning to examine the basis of that discriminating society which has imposed injustice upon him, and to question himself who so willingly accepted it. It has been left too long, however, so that only the bitter, liberating energy to declare war and wreck everything for everybody is left. Most of the workers have not yet got into the way of wanting to take over the riches (i.e. the means of production) for themselves. They would like to, but they don't know how. Baffled and smouldering with rage, and a terrifying historical sense of injustice, they know that to enjoy such riches they would need to control and maintain them – before sharing out the results.

They have not been trained to do this, nor educated to expect it. They are stalled, frustrated, unable to tolerate being what they are, or to make a long revolutionary effort for their own and everybody else's benefit. The men who organised the Somme massacres, and those toadies who attended to the gruesome detail of it, still run the country. The same dead brains proliferate. The same morality governs. The same incompetence rules. Those who see themselves as masters, those who hate the poor because they want to enjoy more of life and are therefore seen as a threat, those keepers of the nation's traditions, the bitter old-mannish intransigents and narrowgutted guardians of privilege, the sham and shallow pontificators in the courts and churches and in parliament, those who accuse the British working man of sloth and deviousness, yet continue to live off his back (little knowing that if they were not on his back he might again become one of the best workmen in the world), those who are afraid of losing what they have acquired by system and not by intelligence and work –

will have to die off or step into the background unless there is to be civil war. The country is creaking fit to crack.

Five per cent of the population owns ninety per cent of the wealth – a more wicked proportion than in any other European country. That is what the old men of 1914 sought so successfully to prolong. That was the victory of 1918, the fruits of which are still being enjoyed, but not by the men who died, and neither by those who survived, nor by their descendants. No Labour government since then has done anything to change it.

The working men of today do not trust those middle class and no doubt sincere socialists to help them and give justice, for they see socialism of that sort as perhaps the last defence of the ruling class against the working class, the only system that will effectively stop the workers getting at their throats. To accept this kind of help might be to lay themselves open to an oppression as bad as what they have now, for such socialists could then say: 'This is what you yourselves wanted' – and what greater tyranny is there than that? We must become each other's equals, and treat each other as fellow human beings no matter what race or colour or religion or passport we have. It is a fundamental attitude that must be stated, but also one which can alter in a very short time if the battle is joined.

73

A mountain of uncertainties makes one unstable stepping-stone across a river, or a single drop of water in the desert. Beware of a man who always says no. He'll enslave you as he too has been enslaved. Look out for a man who continually shouts yes. He'll destroy you before doing away with himself. How can clarity come except out of confusion? How can one decide except through indecision? Seven negatives make a positive. If you dream, you don't act. If you act, you can't dream. That rare and lucky person who does both lives in a world of angels. But he is further from the truth than anyone else.

All roads are set at the truth, whether it is down the valley of dereliction that filters back to the past, or up on to the saddle of exultation that leads into the future. Or take it the other way round, that chaos signifies neither comfort nor satisfaction. Toss the coin of limbo, throw the dice of confusion for any number from one to six. Win or lose, you may not choose, but move you must, until rest is a forceput, and not of your own selecting either. All valleys are exalted, and all hills have good views except when the mists of inbuilt obstinacy cloud them.

It is necessary for every person to explain himself. I do so halfway through my writing life (being if nothing else an optimist) for my own benefit, and as a way of burning bridges. The surviving cinders are visible at the bottom of deep water. It is also a journey, and all journeys are sentimental, whether towards truth, or a trace of smoke on the horizon that vanishes as soon as you look at it. Destinations are illusory, but the point of departure is a mountain of such living rock that you cannot help but set out from it.

And yet, reading what I have written, where has it got me, except to the end of a normal story told in a roundabout way? Wrapped in verbal peregrinations are the lives of several people who stand on an island across the dark and violent sea. From it a light shines, sometimes clear, occasionally obscure. Often it does not show.

All truth is fiction, all fiction is the truth. This book is no more than a novelist's shape of fiction, a misshapen truth, a broad, swamp-bordered Lake Chad whose outlets are narrow flows of myself and little else. I have written about a particular stream, but it is a channel which never expands sufficiently for much truth to be born. If I claimed to write the truth I would have told a lie. If I said I had written lies it would not have been the truth.

It is, perhaps, a historical novel in that people are given real names, while others come out of my imagination. Ordinary people also deserve the benefit of history. And since I cannot guarantee that there is not one lie in the whole of it I have no alternative except to call it a novel.

What, then, is it all for? Life, work, love, living. It is inevitable that I should end on a question, for only questions are divine, the urge to question everything and never take any answer. To accept an answer is to condemn those who provide it to silence, and so you give them tyrannical power over you. The good people in this novel know that you must never do that.